D1594121

HORACE MANN'S VISION OF THE PUBLIC SCHOOLS

Is It Still Relevant?

William Hayes

Rowman & Littlefield Education
Lanham, Maryland • Toronto • Oxford
2006

Published in the United States of America
by Rowman & Littlefield Education
A Division of Rowman & Littlefield Publishers, Inc.
A wholly owned subsidary of The Rowman & Littlefield Publishing Group, Inc.
4501 Forbes Boulevard, Suite 200, Lanham, Maryland 20706
www.rowmaneducation.com

PO Box 317
Oxford
OX2 9RU, UK

British Library Cataloguing in Publication Information Available

Library of Congress Cataloging-in-Publication Data

Hayes, William, 1938–
  Horace Mann's vision of the public schools : is it still relevant? / William
Hayes.
      p. cm.
  Includes bibliographical references.
  ISBN-13: 978-1-57886-363-1 (hardcover : alk. paper)
  ISBN-10: 1-57886-363-5 (hardcover : alk. paper)
  ISBN-13: 978-1-57886-364-8 (pbk. : alk. paper)
  ISBN-10: 1-57886-364-3 (pbk. : alk. paper)
  1. Mann, Horace, 1796–1859. 2. Educators—United States—Biography.
3. Public schools—United States. 4. Education—Aims and objectives—United
States. I. Title.

  LB695.M35H39 2006
  371.01—dc22   2005031179

♾™ The paper used in this publication meets the minimum requirements of
American National Standard for Information Sciences—Permanence of Paper
for Printed Library Materials, ANSI/NISO Z39.48-1992.
Manufactured in the United States of America.

CONTENTS

CONTENTS

ACKNOWLEDGMENTS

This project would have been impossible without the help of two people. Chelsea Durham is a junior in the Teacher Education program at Roberts Wesleyan College. This is the second book on which we have worked. Along with typing the entire manuscript, she has been involved in every stage of the preparation from doing research to the final proofreading. For my wife, Nancy, this is the ninth book that she has assisted in preparing. Her careful proofreading and suggestions have helped immeasurably. I feel extremely fortunate to have had two such able collaborators.

INTRODUCTION

Attempting to trace the uneven and often confusing pattern of development of public schools in the United States is unquestionably a challenging task. It is even more daunting to try to offer value judgments on the trends that have affected this history. Perhaps the most foolhardy effort involved in preparing this book will be developing suggestions that might be beneficial in ensuring a successful future for the public schools. After working in the field of education for almost forty-five years, I probably should know better than to even think about such a project, but I must admit that as I near the end of a career devoted to public schools, I feel that it might now be helpful to seek to study where we have been and where as a nation we are headed with this very American institution.

As I thought about this study, it occurred to me that it would need a specific focus and that somehow it should be different than other books describing the history of our nation's schools. After doing some preliminary reading, I have chosen to consider the development of our schools in light of the ideas of Horace Mann, whom history books have consistently labeled the "father of the common school" or in some cases, the "father of public schools."

Certainly many other people have played significant roles in the evolution of our public schools, but almost from the beginning, it would seem that Horace Mann's work and writings have stood out above all others. This conclusion was made real to me recently while reading a book titled *School: The Story of American Public Education.* The book was prepared by a group of outstanding educational writers and historians, including Diane Ravitch, James D. Anderson, Larry Cuban, and Carl F. Kaestle. Based on a four-part special produced by the Public Broadcasting System, the book traces the history of schools in the United States from our days as a colony of Great Britain until the year 2000. Many educators are mentioned in the book, but unquestionably, Horace Mann was given top billing. Six full pages in a book of slightly over two hundred pages are devoted solely to Mann's vision for the common school. He is mentioned on ten additional pages for his many contributions in upgrading the teaching profession as well as in introducing new approaches to pedagogy. The only other individual whose ideas are prominently discussed in the book is John Dewey, but he was still only allotted half the space given to Horace Mann. A well-known contemporary educator, E. D. Hirsch, is quoted in the book as saying that "Horace Mann is rightly the patron saint of public education."[1]

Those who have studied the origin and development of public schools appear to be unanimous in concluding that Horace Mann was the most influential proponent of free, tax-supported schools for every community. Mann is widely quoted as stating that "the common school is the greatest discovery ever made by man."[2] He was convinced that by educating, in the same school building, children of all religions, social classes, and ethnic backgrounds, society could dramatically decrease social and political conflict. In addition, he was committed to the conviction that such schools would reduce poverty and crime by teaching a common political and social ideology.[3]

After successfully practicing law for a number of years, Horace Mann concluded that the law itself could not create a more humane and peaceful society. When he accepted the position of secretary of the Board of Education in Massachusetts, he did so because he believed that the best way to reform society was through education. For him, the formula for a better world lay in these simple words: "Train up a child in the way he should go, and when he is old he will not depart from it."[4] Among the many benefits that Mann believed would result from quality common schools would be that they "would do more than all things to obliterate factitious distinctions in society" and "disarm the poor of their hostility towards the rich."[5] Contributing to this goal would be the positive effect these schools would have on the growing conflict between labor and management as well as the problem brought on by the unequal distribution of property that seems to many to be inherent in a capitalistic economy. Horace Mann's belief in the value of public schools was based on the premise that as a nation we could, with proper support, create tax-supported schools superior to or at least the equal of any private institution.

Needless to say, there was formidable opposition from powerful interests, but in the end, Mann's vision for public schools spread throughout the nation. This vision includes the creation of schools that are nonsectarian but teach a common morality, are locally managed but state regulated, and provide a tax-supported, free, and equal educational opportunity for all children. Such a school system, most Americans have come to believe, is a worthy objective, which if it were ever achieved, would do much to improve our nation.

Over 150 years have passed since Horace Mann wrote his influential annual reports to the Massachusetts Legislature. Still, these documents, along with his speeches and other publications, have provided the most complete and articulate argument for establishing a national system of public schools. If he is indeed the "father" of our common or public schools, it would seem useful to measure what has happened to the vision of our most prominent educational pioneer.

With this goal in mind, this volume will first examine the background and the content of Mann's plan for public schools. After tracing briefly the spread of his ideas, the major portion of the book is devoted to the developments that have affected his original vision. In doing so, the text will consider, among other recent trends, such topics as the current methods for financing schools, changes in the teaching profession, innovations in curriculum, and school choice. In addition, special attention will be paid to the impact of such initiatives as vocational education, multiculturalism, and academic grouping. Major emphasis will be given to the potential impact of the No Child Left Behind legislation.

The final chapter will be devoted to an attempt to assess the current status of our schools and to suggest some steps that might be taken to ensure that public schools prosper during the twenty-first century. By following this plan, my hope is that the reader will be able to answer the question, Is Horace Mann's vision of the public schools still relevant?

NOTES

1. Sarah Mondale and Sarah B. Patton, eds., *The Story of American Public Education* (Boston: Beacon Press, 2001), 31.

2. Mary Peabody Mann, *The Life and Works of Horace Mann* (Boston: Lee and Shephard Publishers, 1891), 142.

3. Joel Spring, *The American School: 1642–2004* (Boston: McGraw-Hill, 2004), 74.

4. Spring, *American School*, 79.

5. Lawrence Cremin, ed., *The Republic and the School: Horace Mann on the Education of Free Men* (New York: Teachers College Press, 1958), 87.

1

THE EARLY YEARS

The idea that there should be free, locally tax-supported schools did not begin with Horace Mann. Just a few years after it was established, the Massachusetts Bay Colony General Court passed in 1647 a decree that required towns with over fifty residents to appoint a master to teach all children to read and write and that communities with more than one hundred residents establish a grammar school to prepare youth for the university.[1] Although Massachusetts took the first step toward the establishment of public education, various types of schooling evolved, at least for some children, in each of the colonies. Significant differences emerged in various sections of the country during the colonial period.

In the South, which was politically dominated by the owners of large plantations, tutors were hired for the children of plantation owners. Young men were taught basic academic skills along with proper social graces and how to manage slaves. In addition, the daughters of these families were instructed on how to be successful hostesses. Self-taught poor white farmers who were literate often taught their own children, but formal schools were not readily available for most children in the South until the nineteenth century. Teaching slaves to read and write was actually illegal in many of the southern states.[2]

The middle colonies, which would include New York, New Jersey, Pennsylvania, and Delaware, saw the development of numerous church-sponsored schools. These schools were established to accomplish several goals. Often students were taught in the native language of the dominant group in the community in an attempt to preserve the original language of the family. There also was heavy emphasis on the religious beliefs of the denomination that sponsored the school. Thus, in the Hudson Valley in New York state, the Dutch Reformed Church was active in setting up its own schools, while in Pennsylvania, it was the Society of the Friends or Quakers who offered opportunities for children in a number of communities.[3] Interestingly enough, the schools established in Pennsylvania rejected corporal punishment, which was prevalent in most other schools, and also opened their doors to Native Americans and the children of slaves. All of these parochial schools focused on reading, writing, and mathematics, along with religion.[4]

The most important steps toward a truly public school system were made in the New England colonies. In 1789, after the American Revolution, the Massachusetts legislature passed a law that expanded on the legislation enacted during the colonial period. Although the previous bill mandated a community-sponsored school, under the new amendment, the responsibility was lodged with the local towns and not the church. Elected local officials were given the duties that had formerly belonged to ministers, to inspect schools as well as to supervise the curriculum and urge student attendance.[5] This did not take religion out of the schools in Massachusetts, as students were still taught using the Bible and also were required to learn the tenets of the Puritan religion.

Until almost the mid-nineteenth century, support for local schools remained very limited. Even the Massachusetts initiatives did not require a free education for all children, and most families were charged tuition. It is true that many towns contributed funds to pay for the education of poor children. Along with what we would now call elementary schools, grammar schools were established for older boys. The purpose of such schools was clearly to prepare them for the ministry, as the clergy in New England towns were both the spiritual and political leaders of the community. During the eighteenth century in Massachusetts, the commitment of the town governments to provide schools gradually declined. Even though all of the New England colonies except Rhode Island had enacted legislation similar to that of Massachusetts by 1671, by the middle of the eighteenth century, it was the private schools in the largest towns that provided the best educational opportunities. None of the colonies outside of New England "attempted systemic" legislation mandating public education.

Even as late as 1837, when Horace Mann accepted the newly created position of secretary of education in Massachusetts, the goal of providing a quality, publicly supported school for all children in the state was not even close to being accomplished. When Mann began to visit the existing schools, he found poorly constructed one-room structures lacking even the most necessary supplies. Most students were being taught primarily by unqualified and uncommitted young men, many of whom stayed in the job for only a brief period. School sessions were short, with the older children attending most often during the winter months when they were not needed on the farms. Younger children frequently went to school during the summer. It was also true that there was little communication between teachers and those who were responsible for the community schools. As Horace Mann observed in a lecture shortly after accepting his new responsibility:

> In this Commonwealth, there are 3,000 public schools, in all of which the rudiments of knowledge are taught. These schools, at the present time, are so many distinct independent communities; each being governed by its own habits, traditions, and local customs. There is no common, superintending power over them; there is no bond of brotherhood or family between them. They are strangers and aliens to each other. As the system is now administered, if any improvement in principles or modes of teaching is discovered by talent or accident, in one school, instead of being published to the world, it dies with the discoverer. No means exist for multiplying new truths, or preserving old ones.[5]

During his tenure as secretary of education in Massachusetts, Mann visited approximately 1,000 schools. He found deplorable facilities that lacked adequate heating, lighting, and ventilation. There were no blackboards, no standardized textbooks, and the only teaching method was having students memorize their textbook and recite what they had memorized back to the teacher. Most of all, he was appalled by the inequality of the system that had evolved in his state. Wealthy children were in school for longer periods, and the poorest often failed to attend because they lacked even the minimal tuition fees. At one point, Mann suggested that the state of Massachusetts took better care of its livestock than its children. He was also vehemently opposed to the means of punishment being used by schoolmasters, noting that they "crowd from forty to sixty children into that ill-constructed shell of a building, there to sit in the most uncomfortable seats that could be contrived, expecting that with the occasional application of the birch they will then come out educated for manhood or womanhood."[6]

Despite the fact that schools were far from excellent even in the middle of the nineteenth century, the importance of providing a quality education for all children was at least discussed by some of our leaders before and after we gained our independence. Following the American Revolution, one of the most outspoken champions of state-supported schools was Philadelphia physician Benjamin Rush. One of the founding fathers, he spoke out and wrote frequently about the need for publicly supported schools. He believed that our newly established democratic government "created a new class of duties for every American." For his home state of Pennsylvania, this meant creating "free district or township schools that would teach reading, writing, arithmetic and the English and German languages."[7] These schools would provide a common education that would "render the mass of people more homogeneous, and thereby fit them more easily for a uniform and peaceful government."[8] The thoughts expressed by Benjamin Rush would be echoed fifty years later by Horace Mann as he was promoting the need for common schools.

Even President Washington articulated his support for education. In his first message to Congress he included the words "there is nothing which can better deserve your patronage than the promotion of science and literature. Knowledge is in every country the surest basis for public happiness."[9] The members of both houses of Congress agreed in their responses to the president.[10]

Perhaps the most eloquent of the proponents of education for the masses was Thomas Jefferson. While agreeing with Rush on the importance of education in a democracy, Jefferson did not support the idea that schools should "impose political values or mold the virtuous republican citizen." He instead believed that the function of education was to make the common man literate enough to exercise reason and to develop political beliefs. For Jefferson, public schools would also help to identify an elite that would then be sent on to college to prepare for leadership. This group would become a natural aristocracy.[11]

Ever the optimist, Jefferson was also convinced that education and knowledge would improve the human condition. This too would be one of the underlying assumptions in the thinking of Horace Mann. In 1818, while in retirement at his home at Monticello, an aging Jefferson wrote:

> Schools should be established to provide tuition-free education for three years for all male and female children. In these schools, children were to be taught "reading, writing, and common arithmetick" [sic], and the books shall be used therein for instructing the children to read shall be such as will at the same time make them acquainted with Grecian, Roman, English, and American history.[12]

Despite Jefferson's lifelong support of public education, he was not successful either as a leader in Virginia or as president of the United States in establishing a system of tax-supported elementary schools. In fact, despite their belief in the importance of education, the generation of the founding fathers accomplished little in providing educational opportunities for the new nation's children. The Constitution that they wrote and ratified did not mention the word education and did not delegate the responsibility for establishing schools to the federal government. Instead, it has been an accepted fact for most of our history that education was a power that was reserved for the states. Even so, during the first three decades of the nineteenth century, state governments did little in the field of education. The probable reason for their reluctance to interfere with the pattern of local control was that schools had been established and governed by local communities for two hundred years. It would take a generation of strong and committed leaders to establish the role of state governments in providing common schools for the children of their state. Foremost in this group of leaders in the decades of the 1830s and 1840s was Horace Mann of Massachusetts.

NOTES

1. V. T. Thayer, *Formative Ideas in American Education* (New York: Dodd, Mead, and Company, Inc., 1974), 4.

2. James C. Klotter, "The Black South and White Appalachia," *Journal of American History* 66 (March 1980): 832–49.

3. Robert F. McNergney and Joanne M. Herbert, *Foundations of Education* (Boston: Allyn and Bacon, 1998), 48.

4. Peter S. Hlebowitsh and Kip Tellez, *American Education: Purpose and Promise* (Belmont, CA: West/Wadsworth, 1997), 17.

5. Lawrence A. Cremin, *American Education, the National Experience: 1783–1876* (Cambridge, MA: Harper and Row Publishers, 1980), 155.

6. Sarah Mondale and Sarah B. Patton, eds., *School: The Story of American Public Education* (Boston: Beacon Press, 2001), 27–28.

7. Cremin, *American Education*, 116.

8. Cremin, *American Education*, 117.

9. L. Dean Webb, Arlene Metha, and K. Forbis Jordan, *Foundations of American Education* (Upper Saddle River, NJ: Merrill, 2000), 169.

10. Webb, Metha, and Jordan, *Foundations*, 169.

11. Joel Spring, *The American School: 1642–2004* (Boston: McGraw-Hill, 2004), 50–51.

12. Spring, *American School*, 52.

2

THE EDUCATIONAL PROPHET

A brief survey of Horace Mann's life experiences is helpful in gaining an understanding of his commitment to the vision of establishing quality public schools for all children. More than for many of us, his childhood significantly affected his later life. Horace was born in 1796 in Franklin, Massachusetts, where he lived on a small subsistence farm. His father, who died when he was thirteen, left to his children "a strong impression of moral worth, and a love of knowledge." After the death of his father, Horace spent the next seven years working to help support his mother and siblings. He felt a great responsibility for his mother, whom he respected and loved. This was demonstrated in his letters even though members of his family did not easily share their feelings with each other. As a result of this inhibition, this very serious young man was forced to become emotionally self-sufficient. While his relationship with his mother was restrained, he was known by his friends as a witty and buoyant companion. Despite his popularity with his peers, he would describe his own childhood as being an unhappy one. His life consisted primarily of physical labor and there was little time for "leisure or boyish sports." On the other hand, he would also admit that these early years created in him habits of "industry" and "diligence" that became his "second nature."[1]

Along with doing farm work, Horace Mann, like most of the other citizens of Franklin, was an active member of the community church. The family spent most of the Sabbath attending two daylong worship services. Between the services, meetings were held to make decisions that affected the community. As in most Puritan towns, the church was the center of both religious and political life. The pastor of the church was almost always the best-educated person in the community and was looked to as both a spiritual and governmental leader. During most of Horace's childhood, the minister in Franklin was Nathanial Emmons, whose teachings Mann would later describe as expounding

> all the doctrines of total depravity, election, and reprobation, and not only the eternity but the extremity of hell's torments, unflinchingly and in their most terrible significance, while he rarely if ever descanted on the joys of heaven, and never, in my recollection, upon the essential and necessary happiness of a virtuous life.[2]

In recalling his youth, Mann described himself as accepting these teachings until he was fourteen years old. At that time, his older brother, Stephen, accidentally drowned, and the entire family was badly shaken. During his brother's funeral service, Pastor Emmons preached about the "hell that awaited those dying in an unconverted state." On hearing this, his mother groaned in pain at the minister's pronouncement. Horace's negative reaction to the sermon was a turning point in his religious journey. From this day on, he chose to believe in a God of "kindness and ethical integrity."[3] This change of heart would greatly affect Mann's views on the appropriate relationship between church and state as well as his vision for the role of religion in the common school.

The people of Franklin, like those in other Massachusetts communities, did create schools for their children. The parents in Franklin actually built six one-room schoolhouses for their children. The decision to create so many separate district schools was based in large part on the goal of reducing the amount of time children would have to spend traveling to and from school. Individual farmers contributed their own labor as well as free firewood to the local school. They were also expected to pay one hundred dollars per year to compensate a teacher. This money made it possible to have a six- or seven-week session during the winter months for the older children in the community. With any money left over, a local woman would be hired in the summer to teach the younger children. The building that Horace attended was poorly heated and often had a leaking roof. There were few books and the primary instruction was given using a copy of the New England Primer that his parents had purchased for the family. The Bible was the other primary source of instruction. The teachers who came to Franklin were described by Horace Mann as being "very good people, but very poor teachers."[4] These teachers were not hesitant to engage in corporal punishment. If he had received a "birching" at school, Horace reported that he would have faced a similar fate at the hands of his father. Supervision of the school was the responsibility of Pastor Emmons, who ensured that the students were also receiving a sound religious education. The role of the school, like that of the church, was in large part to ingrain in the students the community values, which included "frugality, honesty, self-denial, and obedience." For a few weeks each winter, the classroom joined the "chimney corner" at home "and the pew as a third place of his indoctrination."[5]

Even though the Mann children never had more than eight to ten weeks of schooling each year of their childhood, young Horace learned to read and write at a young age. He credited his parents for teaching him the value of learning, and he later wrote that "they always spoke of learning and learned men with enthusiasm and a kind of reverence."[6]

Along with his parents and his school, another source of learning for Horace Mann was the small public library established in his community. In gratitude for the community naming itself after him, Benjamin Franklin sent to the town a number of his own books, which were used to establish what is claimed to be the "first public library in America." The approximately one hundred volumes were primarily devoted to the fields of history and theology. Despite the fact that they were often difficult reading for a young boy, Horace eagerly read most of the books in the library. Later in his life, as the secretary of education in Massachusetts, this early experience with the community library caused him to propose and establish a number of public libraries. In these libraries, he also included a significant number of books that were appropriate for children.

When he was eighteen years old and still working on the farm, a teacher of the classics visited the community. It was this teacher who convinced young Horace that he should prepare himself to enter Brown University in Providence, Rhode Island. After months of intensive preparation, he was able to gain acceptance as a sophomore at the university. The extensive study that allowed him to become a college student, coupled with his long hours of labor on the farm, placed additional pressure on his physical health. A sickly young man, Horace Mann suffered from long periods of poor health throughout his life and frequently would have to resort to extended periods of rest. As a college student, he spent long hours studying and graduated as the top student in his class. He excelled in Latin and Greek and was described by his teachers as an exceptional writer.[7] At his graduation in 1819, his senior oration was titled "The Progressive Character of the Human Race."[8] The speech expressed an optimism about the perfectibility of people that would remain with him even though he would experience many disappointments during his later life.

Upon completing his college work, he began "reading law" in the office of the Honorable J. J. Fiste. While in Providence, for a brief interlude he also taught Latin and Greek at his alma mater. In order to obtain the best law education available, he decided in 1821 to enroll in the Litchfield, Connecticut, Law School. Two years later he was admitted to the bar and moved to Dedham, Massachusetts, to begin his practice. As an ambitious young attorney, he continued to work long hours and was able to become not only a successful lawyer, but a respected member of his community. After living in the town just one year, he was asked to give the Fourth of July Address in Dedham. Among others that he impressed that day was the future president of the United States, John Quincy Adams. Although he had known his future wife, Charlotte Messer, while he was a college student, as she was the daughter of the president of Brown University, Asa Messer, he did not propose marriage until he was able to support her in an appropriate style. After Horace was married in 1830, he and his new wife were very happy, and a close friend at the time described Horace Mann this way:

How brilliant he was in general conversation! With such sparkling repartee, such gushing wit, but a merry laugh, but never any nonsense. His droll sayings could never be recalled without exciting a hearty laugh at their originality. . . . And then how much power he had of drawing out other minds! The timid ones, who usually hardly dared express themselves on grave and weighty topics, would rise from a tete-a-tete with him, wondering at the amount of talent, thought, and feeling he had opened, and the chord of sympathy he had touched.[9]

Unfortunately, this period of domestic happiness with his new wife lasted less than two years. Her health, which was "always delicate," failed her, and her loving husband would suffer grief that would never be "wholly dispelled."[10]

Following his wife's death, the sad widower attempted to fill his days and nights with new humanitarian interests. In 1827, he had successfully sought election to the Massachusetts House of Representatives. He served Dedham in this capacity until he moved to Boston in 1833. Soon after arriving in Boston, he became a candidate for the Massachusetts Senate, representing his new city. The respect that he quickly earned from his fellow legislators is evident in the fact that he was elected president of the Senate in 1837. As a legislator, he was active in seeking more humane treatment for the blind and the mentally ill. "Almost single-handedly," he successfully sponsored legislation establishing the first mental hospital, which was located in Worcester, Massachusetts. In addition, he was active in seeking legislation that would end the sale of alcoholic beverages and he also fought to end the illegal traffic in lottery tickets.[11]

During these busy years of serving in the state legislature, Mann became involved in the ongoing discussion concerning common schools. As a result, he became known as a very knowledgeable legislator in the field of education. In 1837, Horace Mann was asked to accept the newly created position of secretary of the Massachusetts Board of Education. Today such a title in any state would bring with it excellent financial compensation as well as a large staff to carry out the duties of the job. The chief educational officers in our states today have considerable power in shaping and regulating educational policy. The position that Mann was offered had neither specific powers nor adequate compensation. He literally had no staff available to him to help carry out the work. The only clear guidelines that were given to him were to determine the status of education within the state and to make an annual report to the governor and legislature. Giving up a successful law practice and a leadership position in the state legislature was a sacrifice that most public men would not even seriously consider. Horace Mann agonized over taking the position, knowing that there would be significant opposition to his dreams of establishing publicly funded common schools for all the children in Massachusetts. He was well aware that there were businessmen and farmers who relied on child labor and would see it as an economic disadvantage to have children in school most of the year. The prominent supporters of private schools would also see the tax-supported common school as unwanted competition and a challenge to their very existence. Because of several centuries of past practice, many citizens felt that only the parents of school-age children should pay for education.

In giving up a prosperous law practice for a poorly paid government job, Horace Mann knew that there would be "hardships and privations." In the end, he accepted the position because of a strong desire to make a difference. He wrote in his journal that he was ready to meet his enemies in the "spirit of a martyr. Tomorrow will probably prescribe for me a course of life. Let it come! I know one thing; if I stand by the principles of truth and duty, nothing can inflict upon me any permanent harm."[12]

For the next twelve years, Horace Mann used his leadership position to urge "the ideology of the common school movement as well as other educational ideals."[13] Traveling throughout the state, he conducted hundreds of meetings with teachers and other local officials. A frequent lecturer and a prolific writer, he rapidly became well known as a persuasive proponent of publicly supported elementary schools. Always the diplomat, he did not shrink from controversy but always responded to his many critics without anger or recrimination. During his tenure as secretary of the Board of Education he was able to double the state financial contribution to schools and establish fifty new secondary schools, as well as improve the textbooks and equipment being used in the schools. A major contribution was to bring about statewide an increase in teacher salaries of more than 50 percent. One of his most important passions was to improve the level of instruction, and to do so he was able to convince the legislature to establish three "normal schools" to train teachers. He also argued persuasively that women should be trained as teachers, especially of younger children. In large part because of this support, many women enrolled in the normal schools to prepare themselves for a life in the classroom. Other concerns included school organization and teaching methods. Horace Mann saw the need for a more ambitious role in the field of education for state governments. Although he was quick to talk about the rights of local school districts to develop their own programs, he was not shy about urging "uniformity of textbooks, uniformity of curricula, uniformity of library collections, uniformity of methods, and uniformity of discipline."[14] There seems little question that Horace Mann would be comfortable with the idea of the state curriculum standards that are so prominent in our contemporary scheme of education.

While he was constantly busy promoting education during this period, his personal life changed. He decided in 1843 to marry Mary Peabody, whose younger sister Sophia was married to the author Nathaniel Hawthorne. Together the newlyweds traveled to Europe, where Horace Mann met with many prominent educators. His contacts during several visits would also greatly influence his thinking about education. He traveled not only in Europe but also to a number of other states to learn more about their educational systems. His constant schedule of travel, speaking, and writing gradually wore him down both physically and mentally. Constantly involved in controversy, he worried that his reputation within the state had suffered. His letters now spoke of "fatigue" and "weariness." Increasingly he thought about stepping down from his position to allow a "less controversial figure [to] take his place." During these final years in the position, he and Mary had little money and were living in a two-room apartment in Boston while they were beginning their own family with the birth of Horace Mann, Jr.[15]

It was neither a growing family nor a lack of money that was the most important factor in causing him to leave his position as an educational leader. Once again, his friends urged him to accept the new challenge that unexpectedly became available. On January 21, 1848, former President John Quincy Adams, who for many years had been representing his congressional district in the House of Representatives, collapsed and soon died while participating in a debate in Congress.[16] Upon his death, as a special tribute, the House voted to leave his seat in the chamber vacant for thirty days. This gave the politicians in Massachusetts time to attempt to choose a successor. There was significant support for the appointment of Adams' son, Charles Francis Adams. Unfortunately for his candidacy, Charles Francis had become a very vocal antislavery spokesman, and a number of conservative Whigs thought that his views on this issue were dangerous at a time when Congress was debating whether slavery should be allowed to spread to the newly acquired territories in the Southwest. After four rounds of voting at a districtwide Whig caucus, Horace Mann, who led in the voting in each of the ballots, gained a majority and was nominated. In responding to the appointment, Mann said "with a mixture of honesty and humility" that "to fill Mr. Adams' place" would be a good deal like "asking a mouse to fill the skin of an elephant."[17]

As he boarded the train for Washington, he left behind Mary, who was pregnant with their third child. He also was attempting to complete his twelfth annual report to the Massachusetts legislature, and because he was uncertain that he would be reelected to Congress in the fall, he retained his position as secretary of the Board of Education.

Upon entering Congress, Horace Mann hoped to continue the promotion of the common school but, like all of the other legislators of this period, much of his time would be dominated by the issue of slavery. There was no question in the new congressman's mind that slavery was evil and that it should not be allowed to spread to the new territories. Very quickly, he would find himself in a political struggle between two wings within the Whig Party. Charles Sumner and a number of prominent political figures from Massachusetts were very much opposed to slavery, while the best-known Whig politician from the state, Daniel Webster, would prove to be committed to saving the Union at any cost.

Despite this rivalry within his own state congressional delegation, Mann would quickly make friends in the House of Representatives. These contacts included a young one-term congressman from Illinois, Abraham Lincoln. According to one account, Lincoln found Mann to be "a sophisticated and articulate easterner." Horace Mann's sister-in-law, Elizabeth Peabody, reported that Mann was able to reassure and encourage Lincoln, who was going through a period of self-doubt and depression.[18]

The new congressman quickly began to share his ideas with his colleagues. One of the plans that he spoke of was the establishment of a Department of Public Instruction in the federal government.[19] Thus, one might suggest that Horace Mann would not have opposed the fact that the role of the federal government in public education has been growing during the past half century. In any case, his goal to set up a federal department of education would have to wait more than a century.

In 1850, with a permanent break between the northern and southern states a real possibility, Henry Clay, with the essential support of Daniel Webster, pushed through Congress a series of measures that were known collectively as the Compromise of 1850. Several parts of this compromise were unacceptable to Horace Mann and to other antislavery members of the Whig Party. Included as part of the compromise was the pledge to strengthen the fugitive slave law in an attempt to help southern planters to discourage runaway slaves and to punish those who assisted them. For many southerners, such a law was necessary because of the so-called Underground Railroad, which had been established by white northerners to help slaves escape. In addition, legislation was to be passed to protect the institution of slavery in the District of Columbia. The crucial speech during the fight for acceptance of the compromise was given by Daniel Webster on March 7, 1850.[20]

As a member of the House of Representatives, Horace Mann could not accept what he felt was an immoral compromise that would protect and encourage slavery. He and others from Webster's home state broke with their fellow party leader in a way that would permanently damage relationships within the Whig Party. About the legislation Horace Mann would write in his diary, "How I shall Hallelujah if it is defeated in the Senate!" Daniel Webster came to see Horace Mann as a political enemy. Webster became an even more dangerous opponent when in 1850 President Zachary Taylor died and the new president, Millard Fillmore, appointed Webster as secretary of state. In this capacity, he became perhaps the second most powerful politician in the United States. Up for reelection in 1850, Mann was sure that the word had gone out from Daniel Webster to "annihilate" him. He described his position in this way:

> From having been complimented on all sides, I was misrepresented, maligned, travestied, on all sides. Not a single Whig paper in Boston defended me. Most of them had an article or more against me everyday. The convention to nominate my successor was packed by fraudulent means, and I was thrown overboard.[21]

Despite losing the nomination of the Whig Party, Mann chose to run as an independent and was easily reelected. After this contest the dispute between the congressman and the secretary of state assumed national notoriety. Although Horace Mann's differences with Webster had nothing to do with education, it does demonstrate clearly his willingness to jeopardize his own career for a cause that was dear to him. After 1850, Mann was increasingly drawn into a group of antislavery northern legislators, which included William Seward of New York and Charles Sumner of Massachusetts.

Even though he was heavily engaged in congressional issues, Horace Mann found time to travel on the national lecture circuit, both to supplement his income and to share his views on a number of reforms such as prohibition and the spread of slavery to the territories. While on one of these trips, he met the Reverend Eli Fay, chairman of a committee established by the Christian Connexion, a Protestant denomination that was planning to establish a college. It was to be a liberal arts Christian college without a "taint of sectarianism." In addition, it was to be coeducational, which would also make it very unique. The committee decided that Horace Mann would be the perfect president of this new college, and it offered to pay him $3,000 per year if he would accept the position. On the same day that he was formally offered this job, he was nominated to run on the ticket of the Free-Soil party for governor of Massachusetts. He made the decision to become a candidate, but because he was selected by a new political party that lacked a strong grassroots organization, he was only able to receive 27 percent of the votes. As a candidate, he was considered by many to be too strong in his opposition to slavery as well as being considered by others a fanatical prohibitionist. After this disappointment he decided to accept the position at Antioch College.[22]

His years at Antioch were not easy ones for Horace Mann. The most important ongoing problem was keeping the institution financially solvent. His salary, which was initially quite generous, was never fully paid and was eventually reduced from $3,000 per year to $1,500 per year. Frequently there was not enough money to pay the faculty on a regular basis, which caused discontent and a high turnover. Still, this small struggling college became known as a beacon of liberal thought as it opened its doors not only to women but to all races. Considered to be very liberal in terms of its religious teachings, it still had very strict behavioral rules for the students.[23]

In order to raise enough money to support his family and also to finance the college, Horace Mann once again took to the road as a lecturer, being paid a minimum of fifty dollars for each appearance. On his many trips he was often lonely and sometimes in poor health. When he was on campus, he was very much involved and used his many national contacts to bring well-known speakers to Antioch. Among those who were guests on campus were Horace Greeley, Salmon P. Chase, Theodore Parker, Josiah Quincy, and Charles Sumner. Most evenings the college president would spend talking with the college's one hundred fifty students. Despite his active participation in college life and positive relationships with the students, there were frequent conflicts with some faculty members. The stress of this job took a physical toll on Horace Mann. One of his biographers has suggested that the strain brought him close to a nervous breakdown. In 1857, the nearly bankrupt new college had its first graduation ceremony, which honored fifteen students. Two years later, the financial crisis came to a head and the college actually declared bankruptcy and was sold to a group of Mann's friends. This event broke the ties of the religious denomination that had established the college, and a new board of directors was appointed. For a time it seemed that the college was undergoing a rebirth. Unfortunately, Horace Mann would not live to see Antioch College prosper. In poor health, he delivered his final speech at the baccalaureate ceremony in 1859. His words once again echoed the optimism of his youth when he said, "though evil will be inevitable . . . it is remediable also; it is removable, expugnable."[24]

Horace Mann ended that same speech with the words that would be used as the epitaph on his tombstone. "I beseech you to treasure up in your hearts these my parting words: be ashamed to die until you have won some victory for humanity."[25] A short time after delivering the speech, Horace Mann died, surrounded by his family and students. On hearing of his death, his friends throughout the country would recognize and celebrate his many accomplishments. Today as one approaches the Massachusetts statehouse there are two statues. One is of Daniel Webster and the other is of Horace Mann. At the time of his death, Senator Charles Sumner suggested that Horace Mann's portrait should hang in every public school in America. History has not dulled his reputation. A biographer at the beginning of the twentieth century wrote:

> Mann's countrymen have not forgotten what they owe to him. They have raised statues to him and in 1896 they celebrated the anniversary of his birth; but what is better still is that they remain faithful to his inspiration, and he may be said to be present in their midst.[26]

As the idea of public schools spread, Mann's vision was very much alive as the nation began the twentieth century. The purpose of this study is to explore whether that same vision is with us as we enter the twenty-first century. In order to answer this question, it is now necessary to articulate exactly what Horace Mann believed as he worked to establish public schools in America.

NOTES

1. Mary Peabody Mann, *The Life and Works of Horace Mann* (Boston: Lee and Shepard, 1891), 9–10.

2. *The Dictionary of Unitarian and Universalist Biography*, http://www .uua.org/uuhs/duub/articles/horacemann.html (accessed 13 September 2004), 1.

3. *Dictionary of Unitarian and Universalist Biography*, 1.

4. "Horace Mann," www.famousamericans.net/horacemann/ (accessed 17 September 2004), 1.

5. Jonathan Messerli, *Horace Mann: A Biography* (New York: Alfred A. Knopf, 1972), 12–15.

6. Joy Elmer Morgan, *Horace Mann, His Ideas and Ideals* (Washington, DC: The National Home Library Foundation, 1936), 8.

7. Mann, *Life and Works*, 26–27.

8. "Horace Mann," www.famousamericans.net/horacemann/, 1.

9. Mann, *Life and Works*, 35.

10. Mann, *Life and Works*, 37.

11. Morgan, *Horace Mann, His Ideas and Ideals*, 12.

12. Messerli, *Horace Mann: a Biography*, 246.

13. L. Dean Webb, Arlene Metha, and K. Forbis Jordan, *Foundations of American Education* (Upper Saddle River, NJ: Prentice Hall, 2000), 178.

14. Lawrence A. Cremin, *American Education: The National Experience 1783–1876* (New York: Harper and Row, 1980), 155.

15. Messerli, *Horace Mann: A Biography*, 423–26.

16. Francis Russell, *Adams: An American Dynasty* (New York: Ibooks, Inc., 2002), 243.

17. Messerli, *Horace Mann: A Biography*, 454.

18. Messerli, *Horace Mann: A Biography*, 461.

19. Mann, *Life and Works*, 259.

20. Clarence L. Ver-Steeg, *The American People: Their History* (Evanston, IL: Roe, Patterson, and Co., 1961), 356–58.

21. Mann, *Life and Works*, 338–39.

22. Messerli, *Horace Mann: A Biography*, 539.

23. Morgan, *Horace Mann, His Ideas and Ideals*, 31.

24. Messerli, *Horace Mann: A Biography*, 584.

25. Morgan, *Horace Mann, His Ideas and Ideals*, 33.

26. Morgan, *Horace Mann, His Ideas and Ideals*, 40.

3

THE VISION

It is difficult to distill the words and thoughts of a lifetime into a single chapter of a book, even if the summary is confined to a single topic such as education. Horace Mann wrote and spoke extensively on the topic of common schools over a significant period of time. The primary sources of his vision for education include his twelve reports to the Massachusetts legislature, articles for various journals, his own diary, and a number of letters that have been preserved and published. Perhaps the most logical way to begin a review of his ideas is to reiterate his consistent belief in the essential nature of education in a democracy. The historian Lawrence Cremin has written that

> Mann understood well the integral relationship between freedom, popular education, and republican government. The theme resounds throughout his twelve reports. A nation cannot long remain ignorant and free. No political structure, however artfully devised, can inherently guarantee the rights and liberties of citizens, for freedom can be secure only as knowledge is widely distributed among the populous. Hence, universal popular education is the only foundation on which republican government can securely rest.[1]

These Jeffersonian views can be found throughout Mann's writing, especially in his reports to the Massachusetts legislature. For example, in his twelfth report he wrote, "never will wisdom preside in the halls of legislation, . . . and its profound utterances be recorded on the pages of the statute book, until Common Schools . . . shall create a more far-reaching intelligence and a purer morality than has ever existed among the communities of men."[2]

Along with his unwavering faith in the importance of the common school, Horace Mann had in mind the transformation of the varied and uneven efforts of individual communities in order to create a unified state school system. These new state-sponsored schools would be available free of charge to all children in the state and would provide them the equal opportunity to prosper economically and to actively participate in the democratic institutions of the country. Thus, an integral aspect of Mann's vision for the common schools was for the state government to assume a significant role in public education. In writing about the "three distinctive features of the common school movement," education historian Joel Spring suggests that the reformers all sought the formation of state agencies to "control" the public schools.[3] It would prove very difficult for the champions of the common school movement to persuade local communities that they should allow a bureaucracy at the state level to influence their schools. Throughout the nation, towns and sometimes churches had for decades been in charge of the local schools. The fact that many areas offered inferior educational opportunities to their children did not lessen the opposition to state supervision of schools.

One hundred and fifty years after states began to be more prominent in education, local school boards are still responsible for hiring teachers and staff, preparing and implementing a school budget, and developing academic electives and extracurricular activities. Still, it is true that over the years state governments have gradually taken on the role of regulating or at least overseeing almost every phase of school life. Most important, states have mandated specific curriculums and now tests in the basic academic areas. Perhaps most essential in the early days of the common school movement was the passage of state laws requiring that all children attend school at least until a certain age, which today in most states is until their sixteenth birthday.

Along with the campaign to bring local schools under state control, a second "distinctive" feature of the common school movement was "using schools as an instrument of government policy." Horace Mann and other mid-nineteenth century reformers believed that schools could be instrumental in greatly modifying the social, economic, and political problems of society.[4] In December of 1844, Horace Mann wrote that history clearly demonstrates that great nation-states have all risen and fallen and that if the United States is not wise, it could face a similar fate. He then asked, "Are not the sufferings of past ages, are not the cries of expiring nations, whose echoes have not yet died away, a summons sufficiently loud to reach our ears, and rouse us to apply a remedy for the present, and an antidote for the future?" His response to this question was as follows:

> We shall answer these questions by the way in which we educate the rising generation. If we do not prepare children to become good citizens; if we do not develop their capacities, if we do not enrich their minds with knowledge, imbue their hearts with love of truth and duty, and a reverence for all things sacred and holy, then our republic must go down to destruction, as others have gone before it . . . it is for our government, and for that public opinion, which, in a republic, governs the government, to choose between these alternatives of weal and woe.[5]

Horace Mann also had great faith in the ability of common schools to lessen conflicts between economic classes and religious denominations and even favorably affect ethnic and racial tensions. By bringing to one place children from diverse backgrounds, the fears and prejudices of their parents could be lessened in the younger generation. This would be done by having all children study the same curriculum, read the same books, and be taught by their teachers the same human values. In his final report to the Massachusetts legislature, Horace Mann compares his own views on what is best for mankind to what he perceives is the European model. In Mann's words:

> According to the European theory, men are divided into classes, some to toil and earn, others to seize and enjoy. According to the Massachusetts theory, all are to have an equal chance for earning and equal

security in the enjoyment of what they earn. The latter tends to equality of condition; the former, to the grossest inequalities. Tried by any Christian standard of morals, or even by any of the better sort of heathen standards, can anyone hesitate, for a moment, in declaring which of the two will produce the greater amount of human welfare, and which, therefore, is the more conformable to the divine will?[6]

Horace Mann was greatly concerned as he witnessed the effects of the early industrial revolution during the 1840s. He was particularly worried about the tendency of a few rich capitalists to dominate those who labored. Mann wrote:

> If one class possesses all the wealth and education, while the residue of society is ignorant and poor, it matters not by what name the relationship between them may be called; the latter in fact and in truth, will be the servile dependents and subjects of the former. But, if education be equally diffused, it will draw property after it by the strongest of all attractions; for such a thing never did happen, as that an intelligent and practical body of men should be permanently poor.[7]

It has been suggested that "the life and writings of Horace Mann can be characterized as a constant search for a means of social salvation." He truly believed that "the mental faculties could be developed and shaped to create a moral and good individual and, consequently, a moral and just society."[8] Accomplishing this lofty goal, in Mann's view, depended primarily on the work being done by school teachers "who, by educating children so they would not transgress the law, would replace the police." This concept made schools the central institution for control and maintenance of the social order.[9]

For Horace Mann, the training of teachers was the essential first step for improving schools. In 1838, a wealthy citizen, Edmund Dwight, helped Mann begin the first normal school to prepare teachers with a contribution of $10,000. Dwight insisted that the state match his contribution, and with Mann's strenuous lobbying, the legislature complied with the demand. In doing so, Mann was also able to write into the legislation a provision requiring local communities also to help finance teacher training institutions. During his tenure as secretary of the Board of Education, Horace Mann was able to create three such normal schools, the first of which opened in 1839 in Lexington, Massachusetts. The schools originally required one year's study plus three weeks of practice teaching.[10]

The normal schools included in their curriculum instruction in how children learn, and additional training in the curriculums to be taught, organization of curricular materials, student discipline methods, classroom organization, and a variety of teaching methods. Personally, Mann opposed the method being used in most schools at the time, which emphasized memorization of the textbook followed by oral recitation to the teacher. He angered many teachers by also speaking out against the use of corporal punishment. Although he objected to physical punishment, he did demand strict behavior rules for students and, in addition, expected teachers to be "moral exemplars" for their pupils. Horace Mann was also outspoken in his support for hiring women as teachers in the common schools.[11]

Whether the instructor was a male or a female, Horace Mann appreciated the complexity of teaching. In his very first annual report he wrote that "teaching is the most difficult of all arts and the profoundest of all sciences." He returned to the question of successful teaching in his fourth report, in which he wrote that teachers "need a repertoire of teaching techniques, not only common methods for common minds but also peculiar methods for pupils of peculiar dispositions and temperaments."[12]

In order to ensure that teachers were carrying out the prescribed curriculums, Horace Mann sought the appointment of area superintendents who would aid state officials in supervising teachers. This management function would include, along with certifying teachers, consolidating one-room schoolhouses into multiroom buildings where students would be placed by age in specific grades. While Mann championed women teachers, he did not hesitate to have men as his superintendents and principals.[13]

Along with his ideas about school administrators and teachers, Mann also had very strong opinions on the curriculum that should be taught in the common schools. For him, providing a "moral compass" for children was the primary duty of public education. This was the way schools could improve society. In his own words, "The school room and its play-ground, next to the family table, are the places where the selfish propensities come into most direct collision with social duties. Here, then a right direction should be given to the growing mind."[14] Beyond the responsibility of teaching moral values, Mann believed that the young students in what we would now call elementary schools should be taught reading, writing, and arithmetic. He also believed that music and physical education should be part of the curriculum.[15]

Perhaps the most difficult curricular issue for Horace Mann and the other educational reformers in the mid-nineteenth century was the issue of the role of Christian teachings in the common school. This was especially true in New England, where local governments were entwined with the predominant religious denomination in the community. In all of the New England states, that meant that Puritan congregations supported the use of the Bible as a textbook as well as the basis of religious and moral education. Horace Mann was a Unitarian whose beliefs were certainly different than those of the majority of the Christians in the state of Massachusetts. As a result, he had to be very cautious in recommending any reduction in the role of Christian teachings in the common schools. When he was the educational leader in his native state, some of his severest adversaries labeled him as an enemy of Christianity. Although Mann was extremely sensitive to these criticisms, it was true that religious instruction "had been not entirely but mainly discontinued" when he began his tenure as the secretary of the Board of Education. It is also true that his campaign to end denominational instruction was supported by many "orthodox" members of the Massachusetts Board of Education.[16]

Despite Mann's support for breaking any lingering ties between the common school and denominational religious instruction, the issue remained very much alive in the struggle for gaining public support for free, tax-supported schools. The problem for the reformers was described by Joel Spring this way:

> On the one hand, this meant that if Mann did not advocate a moral education with religious foundations, he faced the possibility of being called irreligious and of having the common school condemned

as a secular institution without religious foundations. For most people during this period, the education of character had to be linked to religious doctrines; otherwise, it could be accused of being antireligious. On the other hand, if he did link moral education to religion, he had to make a choice about the religious tenets to which moral education should be linked. Given the fierce denominational rivalries of the time, any choice he made would create the possibility that the common school might be destroyed by competing religious groups.[17]

As a compromise, Horace Mann supported the continued use of the Bible in the common schools. It would be used to teach "broad religious principles common to all Christian denominations." Mann was comfortable with this, as he personally believed in God. For him, there was a benevolent supreme being who loved all of his creatures. In a letter to schoolchildren in Chautauqua County in New York State, Mann wrote that without God, man "is a wanderer and a solitary in the universe, with no haven or hope before him, when beaten upon by the storms of fate; with no home or sanctuary to flee to."[18]

Not only was he able to compromise on the role of religion, but he also took a similar position regarding the teachings related to politics and government. Here too, he believed that political education should consist of "articles in the creed of republicanism, which are accepted by all, believed by all, and which form the common basis of our political faith."[19] His core beliefs regarding political education and moral values were essential in attempting to ensure that our democracy functioned effectively and that it would survive. For him these values included "the principles of piety, justice and sacred regard to truth, love of their country, humanity, universal benevolence, sobriety, industry, frugality, chastity, moderation and temperance, and those other virtues which are the ornament of human society and the basis upon which a republican constitution is founded." Mann believed that these were "Christian truths" which all rational men would agree upon.[20]

If one were to attempt to summarize the primary tenets in Horace Mann's vision for the common schools, the list would certainly include the following:

- Foremost in his vision was that the common school should be free for all children in every community.
- He believed that the common school should teach a moral code based on Christian principles that could be agreed upon by all denominations. In doing so, the Bible would be used as the chief text.
- He advised that common schools teach students to love their country and to know and be able to use the common democratic principles that could be agreed upon by all political parties.
- He wanted to ensure that teachers understood that teaching was both an art and a science and that they would use varied techniques to meet individual student needs. It was his personal opinion that women were better suited than men to teach younger children. He also insisted that teachers provide strong role models for children and that their personal conduct should be above reproach.
- He continued to strive for a system of certification for teachers, either by a local superintendent or by the state Board of Education. For Horace Mann, the best education for future teachers would be available at state-sponsored normal schools.
- He believed that corporal punishment should be abolished in schools and be replaced by more positive behavior management techniques.
- Schools should be organized by grades in which children of the same age should be grouped together. One-room schoolhouses in which all age levels were taught simultaneously would be replaced by larger buildings housing a number of grade levels.
- In terms of the management of the common schools, Horace Mann sought a prominent role for state government. For him, the state should be primarily responsible for developing a common curriculum in the areas of language arts, mathematics, science, history, music, art, and physical education. Although principals and superintendents would be responsible for the day-to-day management of schools, the state government would be responsible for overseeing all phases of school life.

These ideas, proposed by Horace Mann during the mid-nineteenth century, would provide the basic plan for public schools, which would spread across the nation during the century that followed their introduction. The dissemination of these ideas and the growth of the common school movement will be the subject of the next chapter.

NOTES

1. Lawrence A. Cremin, ed., *The Republic and the School: Horace Mann on the Education of Free Men* (New York: Bureau of Publications, Teachers College, Columbia University, 1957), 7.

2. Cremin, *Republic and the School*, 7.

3. Joel Spring, *The American School: 1642–2004* (Boston: McGraw-Hill, 2004), 74.

4. Spring, *American School*, 74.

5. Louise Hall Tharpe, *Until Victory: Horace Mann and Mary Peabody* (Boston: Little, Brown and Company, 1953), 223.

6. "Horace Mann on Education and National Welfare," www.tncrim law.com/civil_bible/horace_mann.htm (accessed 15 November 2004).

7. Robert Badolato, "The Educational Theory of Horace Mann," 13 May 2002, *New Foundations*, 3 (accessed 27 September 2004).

8. Spring, *American School*, 77–78.

9. Spring, *American School*, 79.

10. L. Glenn Smith and Joan K. Smith, *Lives in Education* (New York: St. Martin's Press, 1994), 248.

11. "Horace Mann," http://people.uncw.edu/smithrw/200/Mann.htm, 2 (accessed 19 November 2004).

12. Badolato, "Educational Theory of Horace Mann," 2.

13. "Module 5: Common School Reform, 1830–1850," at http://asterix .ednet.lsu/~maxcy/4001_5.htm, 4–5 (accessed 24 September 2004).

14. Cremin, *Republic and the School*, 51.

15. Badolato, "Educational Theory of Horace Mann," 3.

16. Jonathan Messerli, *Horace Mann: A Biography* (New York: Alfred A. Knopf, 1972), 333–34.

17. Spring, *American School*, 80.

18. Joy Elmer Morgan, *Horace Mann, His Ideas and Ideals* (Washington, DC: The National Home Library Foundation, 1936), 120.

19. Spring, *American School*, 80–81.

20. "Horace Mann," 1.

4

THE SPREAD OF
THE VISION

In 1850, after Horace Mann had resigned his position as secretary
of the Board of Education in Massachusetts to become a congressman, the common school movement in this country was just beginning. The percentage of white children attending any school ranged
from less than 1 percent in California to 32 percent in Vermont. At
the same time, the percentage of students attending public, tax-
supported schools was highest in Michigan, where over 95 percent of
the children who attended school were in schools financed at least in
part by the state government. Unfortunately, this included less than
30 percent of the eligible white students in Michigan. The smallest
percentage of students attending any kind of school in 1850 was in
the southern states, where approximately 5 percent of the white students were going to school at least a few weeks each year.[1]

The national average for enrollment in schools of white students
(ages five through nineteen) in any school in 1840 was 38.4 percent.
By 1870, the percentage of white children attending schools had risen
to 61.1 percent. The public school movement grew fastest in the West,
while in the South, many of the schools that were available were private. Even in the public schools that were begun in the state of Geor-
gia, only 9 percent of the funds used to finance these schools came
from the public coffers. During the same period in Iowa, 94 percent
of the money for the common schools came from funds contributed
by either the local community or the state. The regional differences

in the development of the public schools were dramatic. Even within geographic sections of the country, the establishment of public schools was affected by ethnic, religious, and racial issues. Many Irish-Catholics and German-Lutherans were willing to pay tuition so their children could attend their own private parochial schools. Until after the Civil War, blacks in the South were, by law, prohibited from attending schools. Even in the North, blacks were sent to separate schools. Religious sects such as the Amish and the Mennonites chose to teach their children at home.[2]

There were also significant differences in teacher preparation in both the public and private schools. Some of the teachers, primarily the male instructors, might have had a university education. Others, almost all female, could have graduated from one of the new normal schools. Finally, in some areas, there were almost no formal educational requirements for teachers. The pupil-teacher ratio in nineteenth-century schools also varied. The 1850 census lists 3,642,694 pupils and 105,858 teachers in America. That is a pupil-teacher ratio of 34 to 1. The same census shows that in Vermont, the ratio was 22.6 to 1, while in New Jersey there was one teacher for every forty-two students.[3]

Even though there were major differences in the quality of the new common schools, the growth of this new American institution was steady during the second half of the nineteenth century. As more people moved to cities, the demands for additional schools grew. The number of cities with populations over 10,000 rose from 12 in 1820 to 101 in 1860. These urban centers all had new industrial and business complexes. Many of the jobs that were created required workers to at least be literate. Not only was the public school movement supported by many business owners seeking educated employees, but support could also be found in groups of organized workers and farm organizations such as the Grange, whose members demanded that their children be given the opportunity to better themselves. These groups saw schools as a possible "protection against the tyranny of the upper class" and also as an opportunity to prepare their children to be active participants in our democratic institutions. At the same time, many middle-class white Protestants saw public schools as being necessary to maintain social control of the masses by

> imposing by institutionalized education the language, beliefs, and values of the dominant group on outsiders, especially on the non-English speaking immigrants. Common schools were expected to create such conformity in American life by imposing the language and ideological outlook of the dominant group. For example, by using English as the medium of instruction, the common schools were expected to create an English-speaking citizenry; by cultivating a general value orientation based on Protestant Christianity, the schools were expected to create a general American ethic.[4]

Common school buildings were also springing up in frontier settlements where they were "often the only public building in the community," and thus they "became the symbol of civilization and the center of efforts to keep literacy, citizenship, and civilization alive in the wilderness."[5]

These western communities led in extending suffrage to more and more white males. Although voting rights for all women in the United States were not granted until 1920, the ever-increasing number of voters and citizens participating in government was also considered by some a significant motivation for communities to extend educational opportunities. Another way that the movement was assisted was the publication of a number of educational journals as well as the formation of organizations that had as one of their goals the spread of public education. Among the journals that were most widely read in the 1840s was Horace Mann's *Common School Journal*. Of the educational organizations, the American Institute of Instruction was perhaps the most influential. Josiah Holbrook was the founder in 1826 of the American Lyceum Movement, which actively presented programs and informative lectures supporting the common school movement. By 1839, there were 4,000 to 5,000 local lyceums in the United States.[6]

Even with the many forces supporting the expansion of Horace Mann's vision of the common school, in urban areas, such as New York City, there was serious opposition. Immigrant Roman Catholics, especially those from Ireland, believed that the common schools were teaching Protestant theology that was critical of Catholicism. As a result, in New York and in other cities, Catholic groups lobbied for the use of public funds to subsidize parochial schools. Joel Spring as well as other scholars have agreed that "public schools in the United States in the 19th century were dominated by Protestant religious values." With this in mind, the governor of New York, William Seward, urged the New York State Legislature to allot funds for Catholic schools. In 1842, this issue became so heated that it caused a riot between Catholics and Protestants. A year later, similar problems arose in Philadelphia. There, in the so-called "Bible riots," thirteen people died and a Catholic church was burned to the ground. As a result of this conflict, the Catholic Church chose to establish its own system of parochial schools to compete with the new common schools.[7]

There were other groups that opposed publicly supported schools. In their book *A History of Education in American Culture*, Lawrence A. Cremin and R. Freeman Butts wrote that "few battles in nineteenth century America were fought as bitterly as the battle over tax support for common schools." Opponents argued that it was the parents and the parents only who should pay for the education of their children. Others held a more moderate position, arguing that tax money should only be used to support education for children whose parents could not afford tuition.[8]

Those who opposed the common school movement for either economic or religious reasons were vocal in every state legislature and in every community, but by the end of the Civil War,

> the major outlines of the American school system had emerged clearly enough to warrant some generalizations. By 1866, the conception of this institution had crystallized to a point where a Massachusetts court decision was able to define a common school as one supported and controlled by the local community, open to all children, and teaching elementary common branch subjects.[9]

Although there was a growing consensus that local government and sometimes state government should finance what we now call elementary schools, the growth of public secondary schools was much slower. In 1880, almost ten million children were gaining a basic elementary education. At the same time, many colleges had been established throughout the nation. Some of these were publicly supported state colleges. The gap in the system at that time was in what we now call the secondary school level. Massachusetts, which had the first college and the first publicly supported elementary school as well, also had the first high school. It, like most secondary schools in the United States during most of the nineteenth century, was a private school that charged tuition. Until late in the century, what we would now call high schools were almost always private academies that were open only to the children of parents who could afford the tuition. Even taxpayers who could accept public elementary schools were slow to agree to pay for secondary schools. In 1874, a Kalamazoo, Michigan, court case ruled that if states could sponsor elementary schools and a state-supported university, it was only logical that they could spend taxpayer dollars on public high schools.

As one state after another began to support a free high school education, the model that emerged was different than that which was prevalent in Europe at the time. In many European countries, students were tracked into specific programs at an early age. It might be determined that they were best suited for either a vocational curriculum or one that led to entrance into a university. "Class status and wealth were often factors in determining a student's future. In the United States "early decisions did not predetermine a child's destiny. The high school became a continuation of elementary education, a path to public higher education, and an affirmation of democracy."[10]

The private academies that had been established as a link between the common school and the entrance into a college originally had a classical curriculum that included Latin, Greek, and arithmetic. By the time of the Civil War, most academies were also teaching geography, English grammar, algebra, geometry, and ancient history. As the nineteenth century progressed, practical subjects such as public speaking and business were introduced in some of the academies. A number of these schools had begun to prepare students both for college entrance and for entrance into the business field or a trade. As a result, the pattern for what we would now call a comprehensive high school was set. At the same time, many private academies moved away from any denominational religious curriculum as they hoped to appeal to a variety of students. A major exception to this was the secondary schools established by the Roman Catholic Church, which continued to mandate classes in Catholic theology.[11]

Even with the competition from Roman Catholic secondary schools and other private institutions, the trend toward public secondary schools increased after the Civil War. This movement resulted from changes that were taking place in the United States during this period. Between 1865 and 1900, the United States changed from having a predominantly agricultural economy to one that relied on industry. As the number of factories grew, there came an increased demand for laborers. Some of the early industries turned to children as a source of workers. Even with the increase in child labor, by 1890, 95 percent of the young people between ages five and thirteen were enrolled in school for at least a few months each year. Fewer than 5 percent of the adolescents went to high school and less than that onto college. Speaking about the condition of education in the United States in the year 1900, historian Diane Ravitch described the status of schools in the following way.

> At century's end, there was no American educational "system." There were thousands of district schools, hundreds of colleges and universities, and scores of normal schools that trained teachers. The federal bureau of education, headed by a U.S. commissioner of education, had no control over local schools; its sole function was to collect information about the condition and progress of education. Education was very much a local matter, controlled by lay school boards made up of businessmen, civic leaders, and parents. State education agencies were weak, small, and insignificant; each state had a department of education, but its few employees had little or no power over local school districts.[12]

Even though in 1900 there were nearly 1,000 colleges in the United States, many of them were more like high schools. Yet, at the turn of the century, public high schools were replacing some of the so-called "colleges" as well as private academies in communities in every section of the country.[13] As this occurred, supporters worried about the many tasks being taken on by these new public secondary schools. The first decades of the twentieth century saw the issuance of several major commission reports that made recommendations on every phase of the high school curriculum. Among the concerns expressed in the reports was the opinion that the new schools were separating students into an academic track and a vocational track. The worry was that this division would undermine the goal of social cohesion that was one of the stated objectives of free public schools.

To compensate for the differentiated curriculum, it was suggested that schools needed to insist on the use of the English language and also include in the curriculum the teaching of social studies, which would place a major emphasis on civics. Another initiative meant to bring about unity within a public school was the introduction of extracurricular activities, including interscholastic athletics. School officials hoped that these activities would not only help to bring the student body together, but provide a way to help control unruly adolescents. Student governments were introduced as a means to give young people an opportunity to become actively engaged in the democratic process. By 1920, the new comprehensive high schools were all working hard to create a cooperative and unified spirit within their buildings. *The Fifth Year Book of the Department of Secondary-School Principals*, published in 1921, includes the following comment on extracurricular school activities: "What we wish the state to be the school must be. The character of our citizens is determined by the character of our pupils and the development of character in the broadest sense must be the goal of education."[14]

Because the new secondary schools included students who were only twelve or thirteen years old, there was a movement beginning in 1909 to separate the students in grades seven, eight, and nine, and in most cases, a new building was built. This allowed a separate faculty and principal for the junior high students. These new junior high schools were patterned after the early secondary schools that housed students in grades seven through twelve. Because in the seven-through-twelve building some teachers actually taught both younger and older students, the teaching methods and organizational patterns used in high schools were also present in the junior high buildings. By the 1950s, critics were suggesting that junior high schools were too much like "mini high schools." A number of educators argued that children in grades five or six through grade eight needed a different type of educational environment. It was their view that there should be a conscious transition for those going from elementary school into a high school program. This would include more student-centered teaching, a closer relationship between a teaching team and the students, separate and more appropriate extracurricular activities, and more opportunities for individual counseling. What emerged was a new organizational pattern that included either grade five or six through grade eight. During the second half of the twentieth century, a significant number of districts either converted their junior high schools into middle schools or broke up their seven-through-twelve building into a middle school and a high school.

Whether at the elementary, junior high, middle school, or high school level, by the middle of the twentieth century, the public school system that Horace Mann had envisioned a century earlier had expanded far beyond what he had initially sought. By this time, students could experience a free education beginning in kindergarten, and if they went to a public college, through graduate school. During this century of development, a number of factors that Horace Mann could hardly have predicted emerged. These trends would affect the strong commitment that Americans have developed to the ideal of a public education for all children. Each would offer challenges to the objectives of the public school. It is the goal of this book to look at these trends and attempt to understand how each has influenced American education. The first issue to be considered will be vocational education.

NOTES

1. Rush Walter, *Popular Education and Democratic Thought in America* (New York: Columbia University Press, 1962), 120.

2. Lawrence A. Cremin, *American Education, the National Experience: 1783–1876* (Cambridge, MA: Harper and Row Publishers, 1980), 178–80.

3. Cremin, *American Education*, 80–82.

4. L. Dean Webb, Arlene Metha, and K. Forbis Jordan, *Foundations of American Education* (Upper Saddle River, NJ: Merrill, 2000), 177.

5. Webb, Metha, and Jordan, *Foundations*, 177.

6. Webb, Metha, and Jordan, *Foundations*, 178.

7. Joel Spring, *The American School: 1642–2004* (Boston: McGraw-Hill, 2004), 103–6.

8. R. Freeman Butts and Lawrence A. Cremin, *A History of Education in American Culture* (New York: Henry Holt and Company, 1959), 203.

9. Butts and Cremin, *History of Education*, 267.

10. Myra Pollack Sadker and David Miller Sadker, *Teacher, Schools, and Society* (Boston: McGraw-Hill, 2004), 295–96.

11. Butts and Cremin, *History of Education*, 275–78.

12. Diane Ravitch, *Left Back* (New York: Simon and Schuster, 2001), 20.

13. Ravitch, *Left Back*, 25.

14. Spring, *American School*, 255.

5

THE GROWTH OF VOCATIONAL EDUCATION

L ong before the beginning of the common school movement, vocational education was occurring in the United States. Soon after the new colonists arrived in New England, master craftsmen began to take on young boys as apprentices. These master craftsmen
were expected not only to teach the skills of their particular craft,
but also assist the young men in learning to read and to do elementary mathematics. In the middle colonies, the need for navigators,
surveyors, accountants, and printers led to the establishment of
"private venture schools." These small schools taught young men
such subjects as writing, arithmetic, geometry, trigonometry, astron-
omy, and surveying. They were established as tuition schools when
there was a need in the area for a specific occupation. The schools
ceased to exist when the need for the vocation lessened.[1]

The goal of having farmers trained in scientific agriculture also
stimulated the creation of Farmers' Institutes as early as 1854. The
Morrill Acts of 1862 and 1890 gave college status to both the me-
chanical and agricultural arts. In 1914, Congress, in one of the first
federal ventures into public education, allotted funds for agricultural extension programs for farmers. Out of this initiative came the
creation of high school agricultural programs in rural areas. Three
years later the federal government became even more supportive of
vocational and agricultural education when it passed the Smith-
Hughes Act, which gave aid to states to pay for the salaries of voca-

tional teachers at the high school level. The law also gave financial incentives to teacher colleges if they would begin programs to train vocational teachers. The impetus for this support was in part created by the popularity at the beginning of the century of John Dewey's views, which emphasized the value of learning based on active participation.[2]

As vocational courses were added to the high school curriculum, the need for counselors, now called "guidance counselors," emerged. One historian described the trend in this way:

> Together, vocational education and vocational guidance assume the function of promoting industrial efficiency through the proper selection and training of labor power. Early junior high schools experimented with ideas about vocational guidance and preparation for the corporate world and thus contributed to the development of the comprehensive high school.[3]

By the beginning of the twentieth century, most educators accepted the role of the public schools in preparing at least some of their students to assume a job immediately after their high school graduation. In many comprehensive high schools, vocational training centered on manual experiences in metalworking, woodworking, and drafting rather than on a specific occupation. In most states, the decision was made that all of the boys in the school should be required to take shop classes, at least at the junior high level. At larger high schools, specific electives in shop were also offered. Girls, on the other hand, were provided classes in home economics. It was not until 1972 and the passage of Title IX legislation that schools opened shop and home economics classes to both boys and girls.

The need for specific vocational education for high school students was encouraged in the years before the outbreak of World War I. There was at this time a concern that German industrial competition was a threat to the United States. As a result, a number of business leaders and educators urged the establishment of separate schools to prepare future skilled technicians. The pressure of Europe's competition led others to the conclusion, expressed in a national report, that children could be divided into two groups. For these supporters of vocational education, there were students who were "abstract-minded and imaginative" and others who were "concrete-, or hand-minded." The report went on to state that "Although traditional academic education fulfilled the needs of the abstract-minded," other students required "highly developed, practical and extended courses of prevocational and manual training."[4]

This approach to high school education has created an ongoing debate among educators. Some suggest that to begin dividing children at an early age into either a college entrance or a vocational program is a mistake. Despite the fact that such a system is in place in Germany and in other European nations, many educators believe that public high schools in the United States should not follow a similar pattern. Cardinal John Henry Newman stated the argument this way: "A liberal education is the only practical form of vocational education."[5] For those who believe that schools should be concentrating on the basic subjects of English, history, math, and science, giving large blocks of school time to anything else, including vocational education, is inappropriate.

Groups in our society that had a stake in this issue were active in trying to influence what was to be taught in public high schools. Perhaps the group that was most concerned was the labor unions. Lawrence Cremin describes the position of unions on the inclusion of vocational education in the high schools as "ambivalent from the beginning." While many unions supported the idea of public school vocational education, there was a vocal minority that pointed out the drawbacks. Some bemoaned the reduction of general education courses, which they saw as the key to college admission and upward mobility. Others worried that schools would prepare too many skilled workers and that this would increase the labor supply and negatively affect wages. A good number of skilled tradesmen were also reluctant to give up the apprentice system, which had for several centuries provided the necessary training for skilled workers. Because individual craft unions generally controlled apprentice programs, some worried about surrendering this power to the educational establishment.[6]

When the National Association of Manufacturers was founded in 1896, it quickly became a strong advocate of vocational education in the schools. This led leaders of the American Federation of Labor to reexamine the union's official position on vocational education at the high school level. Influential labor leader Samuel Gompers became a spokesman against the further extension of vocational education. This remained the national labor union's position until 1910, when it again decided to support training students for specific vocations at the high school level. By this time, "the question was no longer whether schools would offer vocational training, but how."[7]

By the middle of the twentieth century, vocational education had assumed an important role in the public secondary schools of the United States. While there were survey courses offered at the junior high level, a number of approaches were developed for high school vocational training. In many of our metropolitan areas, separate vocational high schools were created. The students in these schools were primarily boys who wished to learn a trade. Although the students in vocational high schools were still required to take English, social studies, math, and science classes, the focus was definitely on preparing them to enter a specific trade or occupation. Because these schools were housed in separate buildings, the vocational students were totally separated from their peers; they even had their own athletic teams and other extracurricular activities. Until recently, graduates of vocational high schools were not expected to even consider going on to a college unless it was a trade school.

Another approach was taken in New York State and in several other states. The state divided school districts into what are called Boards of Cooperative Educational Services (B.O.C.E.S.) These regional boards have as members school districts in a geographic area, which come together to establish vocational schools. Member school districts are allowed to send interested juniors and seniors by bus each day to a variety of vocational programs. Because these programs are scheduled for a half day, the students are in their own school for the other half of the school day. This approach allows juniors and seniors who choose a vocational program to maintain their ties to their home district, and in many cases, gives them the opportunity to participate in after-school activities. Unfortunately, too often, the so-called "B.O.C.E.S students" are marked by their peers as being outsiders and, in some cases, inferior students. This unfortunately continues to be true despite the fact that a significant percentage of these students do go on to further education.

In wealthy suburban districts throughout the country, the number of students choosing to participate in a vocational option is very limited. In many of these high schools, the vast majority of the students are classified as college entrance majors. For many years, most high schools also had a group of students who were not in a college entrance program or a vocational program. These so-called "general students" might have had a major in business or even art or music. This practice has come under fire because these students were not prepared for a specific post–high school job or for acceptance into a four-year college program. High schools have increasingly sought to reduce or eliminate the general education approach and to require that students choose either a vocational or a college preparation option. As more and more students choose to attend either a community college or a four-year institution, vocational education programs in many areas are facing a declining enrollment. This is especially true in affluent districts where most of the parents want their children to go to college.

Still, some sort of vocational education continues to be an option in almost every community. Whether it is located in a totally separate building or as part of a large comprehensive high school, certain characteristics are necessary for a successful program. A list of factors that are essential in an excellent program might include the following:

- The program is directly related to employment opportunities, as determined by school officials in cooperation with occupational experts and other competent individuals and groups.
- The course content is confirmed or changed by periodic analysis of the occupations.
- The courses for a specific occupation are set up and maintained with the advice and cooperation of the various occupational groups concerned.
- The facilities and equipment used in the instruction are comparable to what is found in the particular occupation.

- The conditions for instruction duplicate, as nearly as possible, desirable conditions in the occupation itself and at the same time provide effective learning.
- The length of teaching periods and total hours of instruction are determined by the requirements of the occupation and the needs of the students.
- Training in a particular occupation develops marketable skills, abilities, attitudes, work habits, and appreciation to the point at which the trainee can obtain and hold a job in that occupation.
- Instruction is offered only to individuals who need and want it and who can profit from it occupationally.
- The teachers are competent in the occupation and are professionally qualified for teaching.
- Vocational guidance, including effective follow-up on all students who finish or drop out of a course, is an integral and continuing part of the program.[8]

Even if a program were to meet all the standards on this list, one could still question whether Horace Mann and the other visionaries of public education would support the idea that vocational education was a proper function of public schools. If we think about what Mann hoped that schools would accomplish, the primary items on the list would be as follows:

- Schools should be places where children from divergent economic, political, and religious backgrounds come together to learn about basic moral principles that are agreed upon by all Christian denominations.
- Schools would be places where children would learn the principles of democratic government that were agreed upon by the major political parties.
- Schools would be places that would equip children with the academic skills necessary to contribute to all aspects of their family and community life.

It would seem that to accomplish these goals, vocational students ought not to be separated into different classes. This would be especially true if they were placed for the entire day in a different building. Horace Mann might well have thought that such a system would be too much like the European model and contrary to the objective of giving every child the opportunity to be a leader in his or her community and to be successful economically. He might have been happier with a system that would take students out of their home school for a part of the day. Still, one could theorize that even this partial separation would be counter to what he wished schools to accomplish. This being the case, Horace Mann and others who fought for public education might be most happy with the current suburban model where the vast majority of students are enrolled in totally academic programs. As a practical man, he probably would not have objected to schools offering occasional electives in shop or home economics, while leaving specific vocational training to apprentice programs or technical institutes that enrolled high school graduates.

As we look to the future, one can only wonder about what will become of the field we call vocational education. Will students continue to be prepared as beauticians, auto mechanics, health aides, and child care workers as part of their high school programs? Is it likely that this type of education will increasingly become the role of postgraduate technical schools and community colleges? Will the higher academic standards being sought under the No Child Left Behind Act require a greater emphasis on basic academic skills and cause high schools to eliminate their current vocational programs? Finally, are we approaching a time when all students will need some type of post–high school education if they expect ever to achieve decent wages? Answers to these questions will emerge in the near future, but it now appears that given the demands of the twenty-first century, change in the current system is inevitable. If Horace Mann's historic vision of public schools is to survive, any new programs to prepare young people for the future should not divide students into social classes at an early age. For Horace Mann at least, while children are still students in the "common schools," the doors to their future should remain open to all possibilities. His hope would be that high school graduates be equipped morally and academically to function and to make a contribution to our society, and most Americans would agree that this must continue to be the primary goal of our schools. Whether vocational education will be part of the future in our public schools remains an unresolved question.

NOTES

1. Arthea J. S. Reed, Verna E. Bergemann, and Mary W. Olson, *In the Classroom: An Introduction to Education* (Boston: McGraw-Hill, 1998), 89.

2. John D. Pulliam and James J. Van Patten, *History of Education in America* (Upper Saddle River, NJ: Merrill, 1999), 130–31.

3. Joel Spring, *The American School: 1642–2004* (Boston: McGraw-Hill, 2004), 255.

4. Spring, *American School*, 257.

5. Kevin Ryan and James M. Cooper, *Those Who Can, Teach* (Boston: Houghton-Mifflin Company, 1995), 334.

6. Lawrence A. Cremin, *The Transformation of the School* (New York: Vintage Books, 1964), 36.

7. Cremin, *Transformation of the School*, 40–41.

8. James A. Johnson, Victor L. Dupuis, Diann Musial, Gene E. Hall, and Donna M. Gollnick, *Introduction to the Foundations of American Education* (Boston: Allyn and Bacon, 1996), 448.

6

THE PRACTICE OF ACADEMIC GROUPING

One textbook defines grouping as "a practice whereby students are put into learning groups with others who have like abilities and interests."[1] There are a number of terms used by educators when referring to this practice. One such term currently in use is the word "tracking." Peter S. Hlebowitsh contrasts ability grouping with tracking by noting this distinction: "Almost all tracking is a form of ability grouping, but not all ability grouping results in tracking." A self-contained elementary classroom in which students are divided by ability for an hour for language arts instruction each day but are taught collectively for the other subjects would not be considered tracking by some. The same author would consider tracking to be "the wholesale grouping of students into curriculum programs that result in some identification of high-, middle-, and low-ability (and status) groups. Tracking is marked by the absence of heterogeneously grouped experiences and by clear ability designations between entire classrooms."[2]

Using this definition, it should be noted that tracking usually begins at the middle school level, often as early as sixth grade. In 1990, a third of the middle schools had what might be considered rigid tracking systems. At the high school level in 1990, 92 percent of the schools had academic tracking in at least some courses. The most common subjects where there was ability grouping were English (59 percent), math (42 percent), and social studies (38 percent).[3] Since

1990, there has been a very evident trend that is reducing the number of schools using the practice of tracking students.

The other terms that are frequently used in discussions of this issue are "heterogeneous," which refers to mixed grouping, and "homogeneous," which is used to describe a student group identified by using some sort of criteria. Most often, the factors considered are IQ tests, achievement test scores, grades, and teacher recommendations.[4] Supporters of the use of these criteria in grouping students defend the idea using the following arguments:

- Students will benefit from being in classes with others who have similar abilities because they can be given an appropriate academic challenge. Gifted students will not be frustrated as a result of teachers spending significant amounts of time helping students who learn at a slower pace. At the same time, these slower students will not be made to feel inferior because their more gifted peers are learning more quickly. It is also true that in mixed groups, the more able students tend to dominate classroom discussions. In a group of students with similar abilities, every student has a chance to succeed. Such grouping allows teachers to develop appropriate lessons geared specifically to the class. This will keep students from becoming either restless or bored. It will also ensure that outstanding students will be able to go beyond what is normally taught in a heterogeneous class. At the same time, average and below-average students will have a chance to be classroom leaders and play a larger role in classroom discussions.
- Teachers can prepare lessons that are especially designed for the ability level they are teaching. They can pace their lesson without excessive concern about moving too quickly for the students who move at a slower pace or boring the more gifted ones. Lesson planning will not have to include significant activities that are now labeled "differentiated teaching." With mixed groups, teachers must prepare alternative assignments and perhaps different assessment tools. This is especially true in classes that contain both gifted students and those in need

of special education assistance. With ability groups, teachers can use the same learning materials for all students and adjust the pace of their lessons to the ability level of the students.

- Using academic tracking for talented high school students allows them to take college courses during their high school years. This not only ensures that they will be challenged, but will also save them and their parents money since they can begin their college education while still in high school.

Another individual who fears the movement of "detracking" our schools (ending ability grouping) is Jeff Zorn, who has written:

I picture teaching to the middle, necessarily going over the heads of some of the students and undershooting others. Just by the force of it, teachers will have to spend more time with students who just aren't up to the material, leaving others to teach themselves. I see this leading to what I call the lowest-common-denominator standard.[5]

On the other hand, those who are opposed to grouping have also articulated a number of arguments that question the practice. Such a list might include the following:

- The social implications of grouping can affect the self-esteem of individual students. This is especially true for those placed in a lower group because they can begin to view themselves as being inferior to the students in more advanced groups.
- Rigid tracking can create a social caste system in a school that can divide the student body. Top-group students who spend most of the day together can begin to consider themselves a social and intellectual elite while those in the lower groups can develop negative or lethargic attitudes toward school. Sometimes, there are either discipline problems or apathetic attitudes with these lower groups. For the critics, the potential social outcomes of dividing students is contrary to the democratic principles of the United States.
- Too often, bottom-group students are shortchanged educationally. Teachers have lower expectations and as a result,

these groups are frequently given lesser academic challenges. Such groups also would be deprived of the intellectual stimulation that can occur when a class contains a number of gifted students.

These and other arguments have caused many educators to seek a research-based answer as to whether academic grouping improves or impairs student achievement. Robert E. Slavin, in 1986, did a comprehensive study on student achievement as it was affected by academic grouping in elementary schools. Among his conclusions were the following:

- Grouping students as a class by ability for all subjects doesn't improve achievement.
- Students grouped heterogeneously for most of the school day but regrouped according to ability for one or two subjects can improve achievement in those areas for which they are grouped.
- Grouping heterogeneously, except for reading instruction (commonly referred to as "The Joplin Plan") improves reading achievement.[6]

One of the most vocal critics of grouping is Anne Wheelock, the author of *Crossing the Tracks: How "Untracking" Can Save America's Schools*. In an interview with *Instructor* magazine, Wheelock listed several reasons why she believed that tracking is harmful:

- The criteria used to group kids are based on subjective perceptions and fairly narrow views of intelligence.
- Tracking leads students to take on labels—both in their own minds as well as in the minds of their teachers—that are usually associated with the pace of learning (such as "slow" or "fast" learners). Because of this, we end up confusing students' pace of learning with their capacity to learn.
- We associate students' placement with the type of learners they are and therefore create different expectations for different groups of students.

- Once students are grouped, they generally stay at that level for their school careers, and the gap between achievement and levels becomes exaggerated over time. The notion that students' achievement levels at any given time will predict their achievement in the future becomes a self-fulfilling prophecy.[7]

Despite its many critics, there is one type of grouping that has sometimes proved successful at the elementary school level. Classrooms that contain students of multiple ages have existed throughout our history. It was Horace Mann who brought back to America from Prussia the idea of placing students of the same age at a specific grade level. This pattern has been followed in most elementary schools since the middle of the nineteenth century. In recent years, a number of schools have experimented with classrooms containing students at two or more age levels. Because there is not a clear definition of such classroom arrangements, it has been difficult to conduct comprehensive research studies on the effect of combining children of different chronological ages in the classroom. Even so, Susan Kinsey has suggested:

> In studies looking at long-term effects, advantages for multiage students have been shown to increase the longer students remain in multiage classrooms. Advantages in the academic realm are supported by consistent reports across studies of specific benefits of multiage grouping in the area of socioemotional development. Students in multiage classrooms demonstrate more positive attitudes towards schools, greater leadership skills, compared to peers in traditional graded classrooms.[8]

Whether it be multiage grouping or the more traditional tracking system, the current trend in education has been moving away from dividing students into separate classes because of differences of ability. There is a strong feeling present throughout the nation that every child should be challenged and that with appropriate instruction, all children can learn. In a special issue of the *Harvard Education Letter*, these words are highlighted on the first page of an article on school reform titled "Making Detracking Work."

Evidence is mounting that schools that reserve the highest quality educational opportunities for the "best" students—as determined by a selection process that is often flawed and discriminatory—are denying many students the opportunity to achieve their full potential. This injustice is made even more onerous by the rising importance of standards based school reform, which seeks to hold all students and schools accountable to higher levels of learning. Schools simply cannot embrace high standards for all students without addressing the barriers that prevent many students from equal educational opportunity.[9]

The No Child Left Behind Act does require that all children in the nation be tested annually in grades three through eight in both language arts and math. To many, it seems that if all students are taking the same "high-stakes" tests, it is no longer wise or appropriate to divide them into ability groups.

Other critics of tracking have been even more outspoken as they have labeled the practice as "antidemocratic," "antiegalitarian," and "ethically unacceptable" in a democratic society.[10] Whatever one's views about the practice of academic grouping, it is undoubtedly a practice with a long history in the United States. Even though the current trend may be against the idea of tracking, there are still many proponents who support the practice. The grouping of students "forms a continuum that extends from 'reading groups' (the red birds, blue birds and canaries) at one end to tracking and even segregation of students between school districts at the other." In a comprehensive study whose findings have affected the mainstream of current educational thinking, Gene V. Glass summarized his research as follows:

> More able students make greater academic progress when separated from their fellow students and given an accelerated course of study. Less able students who are segregated from their more able peers are at risk of being taught an inferior curriculum and consigned to low tracks for their entire academic career. Teachers assigned to high tracks and parents of bright students prefer ability grouping. Teachers in lower tracks are less enthusiastic and need support in the form of materials and instructional techniques to avoid the disadvantages of tracking.[11]

The author of the study goes on to make the following recommendations:

- Mixed or heterogeneous ability or achievement groups offer several advantages:
  1) less able pupils are at reduced risk of being stigmatized and exposed to a "dumbed-down" curriculum;
  2) teachers' expectations for all pupils are maintained at higher levels;
  3) opportunities for more able students to assist less able peers in learning can be realized.
- Teachers asked to teach in a "detracked" system will require training, materials, and support that are largely lacking in today's schools.
- Administrators seeking to "detrack" existing programs will require help in navigating the difficult political course that lies ahead of them.[12]

Perhaps the most telling point in the current debate is that although most educators would agree that academic achievement is greater for gifted students who are grouped into a single class, the opposite is true for those who are assigned to the lowest groups. It is these students, who are often members of minority groups, who need the most help in our public schools. Therefore, in order to ensure that all students have an equal opportunity to learn, many schools are turning away from academic grouping, except for language arts and perhaps math groups at the elementary level and advanced placement courses in high school.

One can only guess as to what Horace Mann and the other pioneers of the public school movement would have thought about ability grouping or tracking. We know that Mann was a strong proponent of the Prussian model of placing children of the same age in separate classrooms. This was a major innovation, as the first one-room schools, of necessity, comprised students of multiple ages. Needless to say, these students were also of varied abilities. As with vocational education, there is little question that Horace Mann would have been wary of any "watered-down" curriculum for those children identified as having less ability. His goal was to make every child not only a better person but also an individual who could be a participating citizen of the community and who would be capable of making a positive contribution to society. It is quite possible that Horace Mann would have agreed with the current Japanese model, at least for those students attending the common schools, which has been described as follows:

> The Japanese never group elementary school children by ability, because then different children will receive different educational and social treatment. All children begin in the same class, and the cohort advances together from grade to grade. No matter how poorly a student may be doing, he or she is never retained a grade. Conversely, no child skips a grade because there is no concept of the "gifted" student. Each student is considered gifted in some way. By not grouping or labeling kids, . . . all students learn teamwork, friendship, and taking responsibility for one another.[13]

No one should doubt that teaching a diverse class that contains gifted children, those with learning disabilities, and even those whose first language is not English presents tremendous challenges for any teacher. To do so, an instructor must have command of numerous teaching techniques, be blessed with outstanding organizational skills, and be a person with the ability and sensitivity to work with diverse children. Despite the difficulty of teaching in a heterogeneous classroom, I expect that Horace Mann would agree with the educational historian Diane Ravitch when she wrote these words about academic grouping:

> Some ability grouping was surely necessary and inevitable given the wide gap between the most advanced and least advanced students and the presence in the schools of large numbers of non-English-speaking children. What was not necessary, however, was the idea that the curriculum tracks should provide an essentially different quality of education, instead of a different pace of instruction and different methods. The decision to offer different educational programs depending on childrens' IQ, repudiated the fundamental concept of the American common school idea, which was to provide the same curriculum to all children in the first eight years of their schooling.[14]

One of the reasons that academic grouping has become so controversial is the result of the changing demographics in the United States. These changes have made it much more difficult to implement the vision of public schools that offer an equal opportunity for all children. Perhaps the most important trend that has separated us as a society is the flight of Caucasians from our cities. The dilemma caused by this trend will be the topic of the next chapter.

NOTES

1. James A. Johnson, Victor L. Dupuis, Diann Musial, Gene E. Hall, and Donna M. Gollnick, *Introduction to the Foundations of American Education* (Boston: Allyn and Bacon, 1996), 520.

2. Peter S. Hlebowitsh and Kip Tellez, *American Education: Purpose and Promise* (Belmont, CA: West/Wadsworth, 1997), 397–98.

3. Hlebowitsh and Tellez, *American Education*, 398–99.

4. Johnson, et al., *Introduction*, 463.

5. Shannon Peters Talbott, "Beaten Track," *Markkula Center for Applied Ethics*, http://www.scu.edu/ethics/publications/submitted/talbott/beaten track.html (accessed 17 November 2004), 1.

6. Gary Hopkins, "Is Ability Grouping the Way to Go—Or Should it Go Away?", *Education World*, http://www.education-world.com/a_admin/admin009.shtml (accessed 17 November 2004), 2.

7. Hopkins, "Is Ability Grouping the Way to Go?", 2–3.

8. Susan Kinsey, "Multiage Grouping and Academic Achievement," http://adoption.com/adopting/adopt/article/4143/1.html (accessed 17 November 2003), 2.

9. Leon Lynn and Anne Wheelock, "Making Detracking Work," *The Harvard Education Letter*, January/February 1997, 1.

10. Bonnie Grossen, "How Should We Group to Achieve Excellence With Equity?", http://darkwing.uoregon.edu/~adiep/grp.htm, July 1996 (accessed 17 November 2004).

11. Gene V. Glass, "Grouping Students for Instruction," *Educational Policy Studies Laboratory*, http://www.asu.edu/educ/epsl/EPRU/documents/EPRU%202002-101/Chapter%2005-Glass-Final.htm (accessed 17 November 2004), 1–2.

12. Glass, "Grouping Students for Instruction," 1.

13. Kevin Ryan and James M. Cooper, *Those Who Can, Teach* (Boston: Houghton Mifflin, 1995), 364–65.

14. Diane Ravitch, *Left Back* (New York: Simon and Schuster, 2000), 139–40.

7

THE WHITE FLIGHT

The primary concern that Horace Mann and other advocates of the common school would have about vocational schools and academic grouping is that each might separate children who are from poor homes from those who are a product of better-educated and affluent families. They would worry that such a separation might limit the opportunity of poorer students to rise above the economic and social status of their families. The problem is made worse by the fact that this separation is in large part between white and nonwhite students.

Horace Mann sensed that in his native Massachusetts, even in the mid-nineteenth century, such a division could be a major problem for society. During his tenure as secretary of the Board of Education, there was a growing gap between successful business people and those who performed common labor. He worried about "the hideous evils which are always engendered between Capital and Labor, when all the capital is in the hands of one class and all the labor is thrown upon another."[1] His answer was to ensure that children of all classes, creeds, and races received the same educational opportunity in a common school. Those who believe in a system where this was possible would agree with Horace Mann that "education . . . beyond all other devices of human origin, is the great equalizer of the conditions of man."[2]

As one who deplored slavery during his own lifetime, Horace Mann dreamt of a nation in which all children would have the opportunity to become economically successful and make a contribution to society. He could have hardly foreseen the separation that would so greatly complicate his vision. In the years following his death, the United States continued the industrial revolution at an even more rapid pace. This gradually changed us from a primarily agricultural nation into one that today has only a miniscule segment of the population engaged in farming. At the same time that our economy was changing, we saw new waves of immigrants who also flocked to our cities for jobs in business and industry. Large numbers of former slaves also moved to cities, primarily in the North, where they felt there were greater opportunities than in southern cities. As the populations of the cities grew at the end of the nineteenth century, the result was that neighborhoods tended to be dominated by ethnic or racial groups. Given the neighborhood concept adopted in every city, our schools, especially at the elementary level, were increasingly dominated by one group or another.

This trend became exaggerated after World War II, when every city saw the growth of numerous suburbs. Because the more affluent city dwellers were primarily white, these families flocked to new housing developments that spread out further and further from the central city. With this movement came the need for mass transit systems as well as miles of highways built to make it possible to allow the new suburbanites to come and go from work each day. At the same time that this "white flight" was occurring, numerous farm families were also giving up their family farms to find jobs either in the city or the suburbs.

This "white flight" drew not only people but also many businesses from the cities. As new office buildings and malls began to dot our suburban towns, stores and other businesses in the cities closed their doors. Whole city blocks were abandoned, and jobs that once were important to the cities' economy moved to the suburbs. As a result of this trend, cities were losing their property tax base, which is the primary source of income for schools in most states. According to the 2000 U.S. Census, more than half of our nation's population lived in areas that have been labeled suburbs.[3] Because of their reduced tax revenue, our cities were less able to maintain quality school systems. This problem came at the same time as the number of non-English-speaking students entering our city schools increased dramatically. By the year 2000, fifty-six million Americans, or one in five, were foreign-born or children of foreign-born parents.[4] This influx created even greater educational challenges for our city schools as it became necessary to create and expand bilingual education and English-as-a-second-language programs. Schools also began to face an ongoing deterioration in the family structure, especially in black and Hispanic neighborhoods.

At the turn of the twenty-first century, the so-called nuclear family, which contains a mother and a father along with one or more children, could only be found in one out of four households. Only 7 percent of the households had the traditional pattern of a working husband, children, and a "stay-at-home" mother.[5] In our schools, 17 percent of the children came from homes where the family income was below the poverty line.[6] One in three children was being born out of wedlock. The percentage of African American children in this group was close to 70 percent. Nine of ten of these children were born to teenagers.[7] These issues were by far more prevalent in our cities, where many of our students were living with a single parent or possibly even a grandparent. At the same time, most households included mothers who were working full-time outside of the home.[8]

Overall, the student bodies in our city schools are becoming more and more dominated by nonwhite children. This is true in almost all of our major cities. In the 2000 Census, there was a breakdown of student bodies in the entire nation. At that point in time, the figures were as follows: 64 percent of the students were non-Hispanic whites, 16 percent were black, 15 percent were labeled Hispanic, and 5 percent were Asian.[9] For the most part, the non-Hispanic whites attended suburban and rural schools. In the second half of the twentieth century, our school systems became more racially and economically segregated each decade. In four states, New York, California, Michigan, and Illinois, less than 20 percent of African American children attend schools in which there is a majority of white students. In New York State, only

14 percent of the blacks are part of a student body that is even close to reflecting the racial breakdown in the nation. These same four states each have large urban areas where more than half of the schools have a minority population over 90 percent. Actually, in the South, where in 1954 there were no integrated schools, almost 35 percent of the blacks attended schools in which there is a white majority. Unfortunately, integration in the South reached its peak in 1986 when 43.5 percent of the black students were attending majority white schools.[10] Thus, even in the South, our schools are becoming more segregated.

During the civil rights movement of the 1960s, a continuous effort was made in this country to establish more racially integrated schools. Primarily motivated by court decisions ordering integration, redistricting and forced busing were utilized to ensure that white and nonwhite children could attend the same schools. In 1971, the Supreme Court ruled "that transportation remedies could be employed to encourage desegregation within a school district." But, in 1974, the Court ruled that "suburban schools could not be legally compelled to participate in a desegregation plan unless it could be proved that they took discriminatory actions that contributed to the segregation in the city schools."[11] Other court rulings, as well as a lack of political support for forced busing or redistricting, reduced the number of such programs. Today, although there are a number of voluntary urban-suburban programs for a very limited number of students, little is being done to desegregate our city schools. As a result, the racial isolation in our society continues to grow, and only in a few communities is it even discussed as a problem. The hope of reducing racial prejudice and division by having schools with students that represent the racial breakdown in society as a whole seems no longer to be a priority in our society. The city of Miami currently has only 10 percent of its citizens who are classified as non-Hispanic whites. Seventy percent of Detroit's population is black. Of the seven cities with over one million people, none has a white majority. Our nation's capital is only 24 percent white. In fact, Seattle is one of the few major cities with a white majority.[12]

As the white population and the white-owned businesses moved to the suburbs, the property tax base of our cities gradually declined.

Buildings and the overall urban infrastructure were often not kept in good repair, and our cities have increasingly found it difficult to provide urban citizens services equal to those in the suburbs. Schools were especially hard hit by the lack of a property tax base. (This issue will be dealt with in a later chapter.) The decline was also stimulated by the urban riots that took place in both large and small cities during the 1960s. In 1967, for example, forty-three people died in a riot in Detroit. In 1970, the city was 70 percent white, while today it is 70 percent black.[13]

With the failure of busing as a way to integrate our schools, the concept of school choice was raised as another possible method for reducing segregation in our urban schools. Magnet schools were established in our cities, especially at the secondary level. The idea was to create schools with a particular focus and allow students and parents to choose the city school that their children would attend. A city might have schools that focused on science, the arts, or vocational education. It also could establish an honors high school for outstanding students. The hope was that this type of system would break down the neighborhood school organization and result in additional integration of the races. More recently, the same result has been sought through the use of charter schools. Although there is certainly not a definitive answer to whether choice is succeeding in integrating school systems, one author at least has written that "research suggests that there are severe limits to what school choice can accomplish."[14] The fact is that as our cities become increasingly nonwhite, there are fewer and fewer whites to integrate into schools where the students are predominantly nonwhite.

One might ask, does it really matter if we have integrated schools? Several studies in 1990 found that "racial balance does affect achievement." It was found that

> Segregated schools are more likely than predominantly white schools to be financially under-resourced and educationally inferior, as measured by pupil-teacher ratio, advanced curricula, computers, laboratory equipment. . . . That is, school-based achievement differences reflect not only the race (and poverty) of their students, but fundamental

inequities between districts serving predominantly poor and minority students and districts serving more affluent and more largely majority students.[15]

If indeed our society is not treating fairly those schools that have primarily poor nonwhite students, it would seem natural to raise the question, Why is this not a problem that our society is addressing? If we continue to rely on the neighborhood school concept and do not find ways to integrate these neighborhoods, we will have allowed what one author has labeled "virtual apartheid" to occur in this country.[16] If this is true, it is a condition that our society seems to have accepted. A recent book written by Jennifer Hochschild and Nathan Scovronick concludes:

> Concerns about the effects of school desegregation on individuals and groups have taken precedence over America's commitment to the collective goal of integrated education. That has resulted partly from the mistaken view that there had to be a tradeoff, that equality for and incorporation of the minority could only be accomplished by sacrificing individual achievement of the majority. That false presumption led to an unwarranted retreat from our nation's most impressive effort in the past century to bring the practice of the American dream closer to the ideal.[17]

Others have expressed the hope that because of the growing number of African Americans and Hispanics who have become members of the middle class, we will as a nation eventually succeed in bringing about integration in the suburbs. Along with this, cities will need to continue to attempt to lure affluent whites. These efforts could be very helpful in the effort to create more integrated schools. Up to now, this has not happened, and in fact, the situation is becoming worse each year. The *New York Times* in 2003 cited a study by the civil rights project at Harvard University that points to several factors that have increased segregation in our schools:

- The large increase in black, Hispanic, and Asian students who tend to live in segregated neighborhoods.

- The continuing "white flight" from the cities.
- The termination of dozens of court-ordered plans designed to reduce discrimination.[18]

The fact that students in our schools are separated by race is only part of the problem. Along with the racial segregation, we have a funding system for public schools that tends to favor wealthy suburban communities. The result of this system has been to create what is perhaps the greatest threat to the vision that Horace Mann had for common or public schools. If he were able to tour the schools today in the cities and towns of Massachusetts, he would be alarmed by the differences he would find between the schools in the affluent suburbs and those located in the poor areas in the cities. One could also conclude that he would be equally concerned that schools tended to be dominated by one racial group or another. Horace Mann once wrote:

> I have been taught from my earliest childhood that "all men are created equal." This has become to me not merely a conviction of the understanding, but a sentiment of the heart. This maxim is my principle of action . . . and it rises spontaneously to my contemplations when I speculate upon human duty. It is the plainest corollary from the doctrine of the natural equality of man, that when I see a man, or a class of men, who are not equal to myself in opportunities, in gifts, in means of improvement, or in motives and incitements, to an elevated character and an exemplary life, —I say it is the plainest corollary that I should desire to elevate those men to an equality with myself.[19]

Since segregated schools are a product of segregated neighborhoods, this problem is much too complicated to be solved by any one branch of government or local board of education. An equal educational opportunity for all of our children is a cause about which Horace Mann had strong convictions. He believed that it was the duty of society to alter the unfair aspects of the status quo in order to ensure that all children have an equal opportunity to learn. It is difficult today to defend a system that allows nonwhites and poor children to be educated in schools that are inferior to others that have a predominantly white student body. It also may be true that "although academic achievement for poor urban children was never certain to follow desegregation, it has proved very difficult to achieve without it."[20]

Others would disagree and claim that we can achieve equality of opportunity without integration and that such an end might be the only one possible. Still, one cannot read the writings of Horace Mann without concluding that his vision would be that every common school have a student body that includes people of all economic classes, races, and religions. The issue of integrating races and economic classes provides a formidable challenge for society, but for many, the issue of religion in our public schools is an even more important issue. It is to the proper relationship between church and state that we turn next.

NOTES

1. Lawrence A. Cremin, ed., *The Republic and the School: Horace Mann on the Education of Free Men* (New York: The Bureau of Publications, Teachers College, Columbia University, 1957), 86.

2. Cremin, *Republic and the School*, 87.

3. Sam Roberts, *Who We Are Now* (New York: Henry Holt and Co., 2004), 12.

4. Roberts, *Who We Are Now*, 10–11.

5. Roberts, *Who We Are Now*, 24.

6. Roberts, *Who We Are Now*, 14.

7. Roberts, *Who We Are Now*, 32.

8. Roberts, *Who We Are Now*, 40.

9. Roberts, *Who We Are Now*, 198.

10. Peter S. Hlebowitsh, *Foundations of American Education* (Belmont, CA: Wadsworth Thompson Learning, 2001), 424–25.

11. Hlebowitsh, *Foundations*, 421.

12. William Robertson Boggs, "The Late Great American City," *American Renaissance,* http://www.amren.com/916issue/916issue.html (accessed 4 November 2004), 1–2.

13. Boggs, "Late Great American City," 3.

14. Carol Ascher, "The Changing Face of Racial Isolation and Desegregation in Urban Schools," *ERIC/CUE Digest*, http://www.ericdigests.org/1993/face.htm (accessed 4 October 2004), 2.

15. Ascher, "Changing Face," 4.

16. Lawrence Hardy, "The New Dive," *American School Board Journal*, http://64.233.161.104/search?q=cache:We0m49GBcIJ:www.asbj.com/Brown vBoard/0404m, April 2004 (accessed 4 October 2004), 2.

17. Jennifer Hochschild and Nathan Scovronick, *The American Dream and the Public Schools* (New York: Oxford University Press, 2003), 50–51.

18. Hardy, "The New Dive," 2.

19. Joy Elmer Morgan, *Horace Mann, His Ideas and Ideals* (Washington, DC: National Home Library Foundation, 1936), 124.

20. Hochschild and Scovronick, *American Dream*, 51.

8

THE CHURCH
AND STATE ISSUE

Since the first days of the movement to create common or public schools, the debate on the role of religion in education has not abated. At the time that Horace Mann was seeking to persuade the people of Massachusetts to accept the idea of tax-supported schools, most of the existing schools in all of the states were directly affiliated with one of the Christian denominations. Many community leaders as well as members of the various sponsoring churches were worried that the new public schools would cause their own schools to cease to exist. Others were sincerely concerned that the new common schools would be devoid of any religious teaching and that they would be godless institutions managed by far-off state bureaucrats. Horace Mann and other common school advocates were forced to deal with this opposition, which was often articulated by prominent clergymen.

As a result of this active opposition, the proponents of tax-supported schooling had to develop a position that would gain majority support, even though some people would always be opposed to any compromise on the religious issue. During the debate, Horace Mann was frequently labeled as an individual who lacked a true commitment to Christianity. It is true, as we have seen, that Mann at an early age gave up the fundamentalist views of his earliest church. As a result, it is not surprising that he should have written about this change in his views as follows:

> I remember the day, the hour, the place and the circumstances, as well as though the event had happened but yesterday, when in an agony of despair, I broke the spell that bound me. From that day, I began to construct the theory of Christian ethics and doctrine respecting virtue and vice, rewards and penalties, time and eternity, God and His providence, which . . . I still retain.[1]

Soon after rejecting his early Christian teachings, Mann was greatly affected by the sermons and writings of the Unitarian minister William Ellery Channing. One biographer suggests that Channing was influential in helping Mann to put behind him the tragedy of the death of his first wife, Charlotte.[2] Although he may not have personally accepted all of the details of the Christian creed, one would conclude from his writings and speeches that he believed in a loving and benevolent God. In writing about teaching children, he specifically noted that instruction should

> give them a delight in exploring the vast world of natural history, where, at every step, they are surrounded by proofs of the greatness and goodness of God; and thus to prepare them, as far as by any human means they can be prepared, to bring a clear and stronger mind and less selfish and impure affections, a more ardent love of man and a higher reverence for God.[3]

Mann begins his often-quoted *Twelfth Report to the Massachusetts Board of Education* with the words "Under the providence of God." He devotes a major section of this, his final report, to the subject of religious education. In this section, he makes clear his ardent admiration for the moral teachings of Christianity as they are articulated in the Bible. He writes explicitly that he has never sought to exclude "either the Bible or religious instruction from the schools." He believes that the Bible can help to teach what he considers the true Christian virtues. The qualities he lists in his report include "piety, justice, and a sacred regard to truth, love to their country, humanity and universal benevolence, sobriety, industry, and frugality, chastity, moderation, and temperance." He asks, "Are not these virtues and graces part and parcel of Christianity?"[4] He goes on to argue that those who charge that common schools are anti-Christian are admitting that their Christianity would not affirm this list of virtues.[5]

The reason that Mann felt it was necessary to focus on what he believed to be virtues that could be agreed upon by all Christians was that he thought that it was crucial to break the control that individual denominations might have over their local schools. He portrayed what could happen if this was allowed to continue:

> Suppose they do have sectarian teaching in the schools, . . . and local school boards . . . should decide from year to year and depending on their personal preferences, what religion should be taught in the schools! One sect may have ascendancy today; another tomorrow. This year there will be Three persons in the Godhead; next year but One . . . this year the everlasting fires of hell will burn to terrify the impenitent; next year, and without any repentance, the eternal flames will be rekindled forever, or quenched forever—as it may be decided in town meeting! This year the ordinance of baptism will be inefficacious without immersion; next year one drop of water will be as good as forty fathoms. Children attending district school will be taught one way; going from district school to high school will be taught another.[6]

Although Mann and all of the earlier supporters of common schools were worried about denominational control, Mann's commitment to teaching positive Christian values can be seen in this comment about the selection of teachers. In a letter from the Reverend D. Wright Jun in 1848, Mann was asked if "literary qualifications are alone sufficient for those who would be a teacher." His answer was that they were not. For Horace Mann, "Moral qualifications, and the ability to inculcate and enforce the Christian virtues, I consider to be even of greater moment than literary attainments."[7]

Because many saw Horace Mann's religious views as being those of a Protestant Christian, there were questions about whether a Roman

Catholic child or teacher could be comfortable in his vision of the common school. In answer to the question about the possibility of Catholic teachers, he responded, "I do not see how, according to our law, a man is to be disfranchised, or held to be disqualified for the office of a teacher, merely because he is a Catholic."[8]

Needless to say, many Catholics would not feel comfortable sending their children to the public schools that were founded on Mann's religious model. The same would be true of many Jewish families. Still politically, given the domination of those affiliated with Protestant churches, probably no other approach would have been as effective in gaining widespread support for the common school movement. Horace Mann's religious compromise remained in place for over a century. It is undoubtedly true that the practice of teaching agreed-upon Christian virtues using the Bible decreased in importance in nearly all public schools in the century following Mann's work in Massachusetts. Still, as late as the 1950s, students and faculty were praying together in public schools. School assemblies might often begin with a prayer or scripture reading. As early as 1925, the Supreme Court began to reduce the flexibility of state governments in the area of religion. That year, in the state of Oregon, a law requiring that all children without exception attend a public school was ruled unconstitutional because it "denied due process of law by taking from parents their freedom to direct the upbringing and education of their children by sending them either to parochial or private non-sectarian schools of approved educational standards."[9] On the other hand, the court ruled in *McCollum v. Maryland* in 1948 that schools could, if requested by local churches, allow release time for religious education at a site other than a school building.[10]

The key case that affected the role of religion in schools was *Engel v. Vitale* in 1962. The state board of education in New York, known as the Board of Regents, was requiring that a nondenominational prayer be read each day in every public school in the state. The wording of the prayer was as follows: "Almighty God, we acknowledge our dependence upon Thee, and we beg Thy blessings upon us, our parents, our teachers and our Country."[11] The ten parents who objected to the prayer and challenged it in the federal

courts included Jews, Unitarians, Ethical Culturalists, and nonbe-
lievers. Their lawyers claimed that the prayer requirement "was contrary to the beliefs, religions, or religious practices of themselves
and their children." After declaring the so-called Regents prayer unconstitutional, the court would go on in the cases of *Abbington
School District v. Schempp* and *Murray v. Curlett* to declare the practice of reading from the Bible and reciting the Lord's Prayer unconstitutional.[12]

Justice William O. Douglas, a member of the court when these decisions were written, justified the thinking of the justices when he
wrote that the heritage that the public schools should

> seek to instill is one that all sects, all races, all groups have in com-
> mon. It is not atheistic nor is it theistic. It is a civic and patriotic her-
> itage that transcends all differences among people, that bridges the
> gaps in sectarian creeds, that cements all in a common unity of na-
> tionality, and that reduces differences that emphasis on race, creed,
> and sect only accentuate.[13]

It is likely that Horace Mann would have been alarmed by the decision to take prayer and the Bible out of the public schools, but he
certainly would have agreed with what Justice Douglas wrote about
the purpose of these schools.

There have been many other important decisions regarding the
role of religion in our public schools. To help school officials and
the courts determine what is a legal practice in our schools, the
Supreme Court, in the case of *Lemon v. Kurtzman* in 1971, established a three-part test. The questions to be asked about any policy
were, does this policy or practice have a secular purpose, does it
have a primarily secular effect, and does it avoid excessive government entanglements with religion? Using this test, a one-minute
moment of silence for meditation or voluntary prayer was declared
unconstitutional. More recent decisions seem to have given more
latitude to schools engaging in this practice. A Kentucky policy that
required the posting of the Ten Commandments in every classroom
has also been struck down. The issue of saying a prayer during
a high school graduation remains somewhat unclear. Currently a

student-led, nondenominational prayer, which is supported by the senior class, appears to be acceptable.[14]

Perhaps the most heated of the constitutional issues regarding schools and religion is the teaching of evolution. The legal controversy began in 1925 with the trial of John Scopes, a Tennessee biology teacher who chose to violate a state statute that made it illegal to teach about the theory of evolution. Because of the participation of Democratic political leader William Jennings Bryan as the prosecutor and the famous attorney Clarence Darrow, who acted in defense of Scopes, the event took on national and international importance. It gained even further attention from a play and a movie titled *Inherit the Wind*. Although the teacher was found guilty and the law remained in place, the continuing battle between fundamentalist Christians and many leaders of the science community had begun.[15]

It was not until 1968 that the Supreme Court affirmed the right to teach evolution in the public schools, even though most schools had already included evolution in their science curriculums. Although state courts in the 1980s did allow schools to give equal instructional time to biblical creationism, the Supreme Court ruled in *Edwards v. Aquillard* in 1987 that policies requiring instruction in creationism are a violation of the First Amendment.[16]

The fact is that the conflict between creationism and evolution has not lessened. In October of 2004, the *Washington Post* carried a story describing a debate taking place among board members of the Charles County Board of Education in southern Maryland. There, the board of education has compiled a list of goals for improving the school system. Among these goals are instituting the practice of "distributing Bibles in schools and removing science books which are biased toward evolution." A representative of the Charles County teacher organization has charged that those supporting these goals are "trying to skew the curriculum, to teach their own conservative Christian values." It should be noted that the practice of allowing the Gideon Society to distribute Bibles in schools has already been declared unconstitutional.

Despite the numerous restrictions on religious activities in school, it is possible that as the makeup of our federal court judiciary becomes more conservative, some previous decisions will be modified or overturned. The emotions engendered by these issues can be seen in a quote from the *Washington Post* in which a guidance counselor in the district said, "Basically, these people are telling you how you should be and, if you're not, you're a bad person . . . if this is what they're going to do, I'll pull my kids out of school and teach them myself." A tenth-grade biology teacher was also very vehement when he told the *Post* reporter that "supernatural beliefs simply don't belong in a science class. . . . We deal with the scientific evidence available. If they bring this into a science curriculum and want to talk about evidence, I'll rip it to shreds."[17]

As the practice of teaching Christianity in schools became less possible, educators sought to find ways to instruct students in morality and values using methods that are not tied directly to the Bible. The result has been a series of approaches that have sought to help students make positive moral decisions. One approach is called "values clarification." It is a program designed to assist students to develop their own values system. Critics say that the approach "treats all values equally" and is in reality "value neutral." Values clarification has become somewhat controversial and has been banned in some school districts.[18]

A second plan, adopted by many districts, is called character education. More than half of the states have required such a program in their public schools. Although there are various ways to carry out character education, each assumes "that there are core attributes of a moral individual that children should be directly taught in school." Such values include characteristics such as "trustworthiness, respect, responsibility, fairness, caring, and good citizenship." Instructional approaches include the use of appropriate literature, utilizing examples from history, and the teaching of conflict resolution skills. As might be expected, there are those who see character education as "superficial, artificially forcing a diverse student population into a simplistic and narrow set of unexamined values that do not really alter behaviors."[19] A third approach relies on the work of psychologist Jean Piaget. Formulated by Lawrence Kohlberg, the so-called "moral stages of development" are used as the basis of a strategy for teaching right and wrong. In young children, rewards and punishment are used. As children mature, the hope is that they will accept the laws and even go on to question the validity of the rules of society. As part of Kohlberg's curriculum, students are encouraged to analyze moral dilemmas presented in brief scenarios.

For example, one such scenario might tell the story of someone breaking into a store and stealing, and the question is posed: Isn't stealing always wrong, or could it ever be justified? What if the person was stealing medicine needed to save a life; would that justify the theft? The teacher's role in this curriculum is to help students move to higher stages of moral development.[20]

While some schools have reported a decline of discipline problems as a result of their efforts in the field of values education, there is no conclusive evidence to support the effectiveness of these programs. Even without such research, the federal government has invested over $50,000,000 to help fund such programs. In a book published by Teachers College at Columbia University in 1998, Richard A. Baer raises the question, "Is it possible to teach morality and character education effectively in our present system of public schools in America?"[21] At the end of his discussion, he frames the issue this way:

Will we, in the tradition of Horace Mann, side with the National Education Association in supporting a monopoly system of government schools that are fundamentally vehicles for one or another cultural elite to exercise social control, or will we, in the spirit of the First Amendment's religion clause, endorse school disestablishment and view the state's role in education as the guarantor of just access to education rather than that of religious mentor or moral tutor?[22]

Baer and others believe that given our current diversity as a nation, we cannot agree on a common set of moral values to be taught in our schools. In other words, the vision of Horace Mann's common school, in which all Americans are taught a common moral code, is no longer possible. Many other individuals would argue that it is more necessary than ever that we attempt to create among our children and our people a core of shared knowledge and values. Two current trends that are testing whether the vision of Horace Mann will remain paramount are the current issues of multicultural education and school choice. In the next chapter we will consider the impact of multicultural thinking on our public schools.

NOTES

1. Jonathan Messerli, *Horace Mann: A Biography* (New York: Alfred A. Knopf, 1972), 20.

2. Messerli, *Horace Mann: A Biography*, 179–80.

3. Joy Elmer Morgan, *Horace Mann, His Ideas and Ideals* (Washington, DC: The National Home Library Foundation, 1936), 134.

4. Lawrence A. Cremin, ed., *The Republic and the School: Horace Mann on the Education of Free Men* (New York: Bureau of Publications, Teachers College, Columbia University, 1957), 106.

5. Cremin, *Republic and the School*, 107.

6. Louise Hall Tharp, *Until Victory* (Boston: Little, Brown and Company, 1953), 206.

7. Mary Peabody Mann, *The Life and Works of Horace Mann* (Boston: Lee and Shepard Publishers, 1891), 262.

8. Mann, *Life and Works*, 263.

9. Robert E. Cushman and Robert F. Cushman, *Cases in Constitutional Law* (New York: Appleton-Century-Crofts, Inc., 1958), 444.

10. Myra Pollack Sadker and David Miller Sadker, *Teachers, Schools, and Society, Seventh Edition*, (Boston: McGraw-Hill, 2004), 414.

11. William O. Douglas, *The Bible and the Schools* (Boston: Little, Brown, and Company, 1966), 17.

12. Douglas, *Bible and the Schools*, 17–18.

13. Douglas, *Bible and the Schools*, 58–59.

14. Sadker and Sadker, *Teachers, Schools, and Society*, 414.

15. Boyd C. Shafer, Richard A. McLemore, and Everett Augspurger, *United States History* (River Forest, IL: Laidlaw Brothers Publishers, 1969), 540.

16. Sadker and Sadker, *Teachers, Schools, and Society*, 414.

17. Joshua Partlow, "School Board Considers Censoring Books, Handing Out Bibles, Teaching Creation," *Washington Post,* 10 October 2004, www.washingtonpost.com/wp-dyn/articles/A20713-2004Oct9.html (accessed 15 October 2004), 3.

CHAPTER 8

18. Sadker and Sadker, *Teachers, Schools, and Society*, 418.

19. Sadker and Sadker, *Teachers, Schools, and Society*, 419.

20. Sadker and Sadker, *Teachers, Schools, and Society*, 420.

21. James T. Sears, ed., *Curriculum, Religion, and Public Education* (New York: Teachers College Press, 1998), 105.

22. Sears, *Curriculum*, 113.

9

THE
MULTICULTURAL ISSUE

Many historians of American education would agree with the conclusion of Joel Spring, who wrote in a recent book that "a major part of the history of U.S. public schools is the attempt to ensure the domination of a Protestant Anglo-American culture in the United States."[1] Spring traces the struggle for cultural domination to the early English colonists. Several centuries later, during the lifetime of Horace Mann, the control of schools and other institutions was being challenged, especially by the waves of Irish-Catholic immigrants, who would soon be joined by other groups, including African Americans and Native Americans.

Very likely, one reason Mann and others were successful in persuading white Protestant taxpayers to support public schools was the hope that such schools would be instructing all students in the values that were accepted by the dominant Protestant Anglo-American culture. Although Horace Mann would not have thought of his goals in this way, he was unquestionably attempting to establish a public school system that would teach what he considered Christian values as well as an understanding and reverence for democracy and capitalism. In seeking this goal, his vision was shared by the majority of the American taxpayers during his lifetime and well into the twentieth century. Even so, there were, from the beginning of the fight for common schools, a number of Roman Catholics and other Christians who concluded that these tax-supported schools would not provide an appropriate education for their children. Because of this fact, competing parochial school systems, which include a significant number of schools sponsored by various Christian denominations, have continued to exist as competitors to the public school system.

Early in the twentieth century, there began an ongoing discussion of the need to diversify our approach to education in the public schools. As early as 1915, Horace Callen wrote about a concept that he labeled "cultural pluralism." He used the term to describe "a new kind of polity and a new kind of public education, in which a variety of cultures besides that of England and English influenced America would receive a significant place in American education." In 1998, the term was still being used. In writing about cultural pluralism, McNergney and Herbert defined it as "a state in which people of diverse ethnic, racial, religious, and social groups maintain autonomous participation within a common civilization."[2]

Prior to these discussions, most Americans thought of their schools as a place where all children would be assimilated into our common culture. Thus, our schools were thought of as a major contributor to what was called the "melting pot," which was creating Americans from a population that was growing increasingly diverse. It was not until the 1960s that this point of view was seriously challenged. During these years

> African-Americans, Hispanics, Native Americans and other racial and ethnic groups continued to experience discrimination, and attempts to increase upward mobility of children from poor families were generally unsuccessful. Thus, during the 1960's, concurrent with the civil rights-movement, the concept of cultural pluralism replaced the assimilation concept.[3]

At the same time, women in America began to mobilize to ensure that they could become equal beneficiaries in our society. Colleges and universities began individual courses in departments in areas known as Women's Studies and Black Studies. Numerous authors began to point to the fact that our school curriculums in history, music, art, and literature were devoted almost totally to "dead, white, European males" (DWEMs). Critics began to call for an educational program that provided "a balanced appreciation and critique of other cultures as well as our own."[4]

In recent years, the term "multicultural education" has become the label for efforts to diversify the school curriculum. The best-known leader in this field is James A. Banks. He has written that multicultural education has the all-encompassing goal to "transform the school so that male and female students, exceptional students, and students from diverse cultural, social class, racial, and ethnic groups experience an equal opportunity to learn." In order to do this, schools must achieve in the classroom a "climate" that "is more consistent with diverse cultures and learning styles." Justification for the need to accept this point of view is based on the research of Carol Gilligan and others, who have isolated differences in the way certain groups learn.[5]

Along with emphasizing the need to be cognizant of varied learning styles, Banks has also identified ways to integrate the curriculum and make it more inclusive. He has developed a taxonomy of approaches that includes the following:

- *Contribution Approach*—Textbook publishers, when pressed, inserted pages into their standard history texts to highlight contributions of people like Susan B. Anthony and Frederick Douglass. Another approach would be to add to the school schedule a day to celebrate the contributions of Native Americans. This could include allowing the students to prepare special foods or experience Native American art or music.
- *Additive Approach*—An entire month might be dedicated to the contributions of one group or another: for instance, Black History Month or Women's History Month.
- *Transformational Approach*—"The entire Euro-centric nature of the curriculum is changed. Students are taught to view events and issues from diverse, ethnic, and cultural perspectives. For instance, the westward expansion of Europeans can be seen as 'manifest destiny' through the eyes of European descendents or as an invasion from the East, through the eyes of Native Americans."

- *Social Action*—Teachers or schools would have the students become involved in solving social problems. This could include a class letter-writing campaign to affect legislation that would help fund United Nations humanitarian agencies.[6]

One of the problems in attempting to understand multicultural education is determining what the objectives should be. Despite the difficulty of articulating the specific goals of the movement, certain assumptions seem to be shared by all of its advocates:

- Multiculturalism values cultural pluralism and seeks to have students celebrate their ancestry and our nation's diversity.
- Multiculturalism has as a major objective the reduction of prejudice and the creation of tolerance.
- Multiculturalism utilizes knowledge of varied learning styles in order to improve the academic performance of minority students.
- Multicultural education is an attempt to incorporate into the curriculum the contribution and points of view of those groups that have been all but ignored in the past. This should be done not only in history classes but in the curriculums of English, music, and art classes.[7]

Multiculturalism calls for replacing the "melting pot" approach in our schools with the "mosaic" or "tossed salad" model, where "individual parts are distinct but combined to make a unique whole." In a publication of the American Association of Colleges for Teacher Education, the goal of multicultural education should be to

> endorse the principle that there is no one model American. . . . [and] to understand and appreciate the differences that exist among the nation's citizens. It is to see these differences as a positive force. . . . Cultural pluralism is more than a temporary accommodation to placate racial and ethnic minorities. It is a concept that aims toward a heightened sense of being and of wholeness of the entire society based on the unique strengths of each of its parts.[8]

Banks defends such an approach, saying that it will not only have a positive effect on unrepresented minorities but will also "restructure educational institutions so that all students, including middle-class white males, will acquire the knowledge, skills, and attitudes needed to function effectively in a culturally and ethnically diverse nation and world."[9] The supporters of multicultural education are cautiously optimistic about its success to date. They can point to a number of books, conferences, courses in schools of education, and curriculum modifications that have taken place throughout the nation. Publishers have also become extremely sensitive to their concerns. Integration of the contributions of minorities into the regular text is replacing the one-page insert that highlights a minority individual. Students are reading a wider variety of authors, and music majors are taking courses that deal with various music styles. At the same time, Banks warns his fellow multiculturalists that there is a

> highly organized, well-financed attack by Western traditionalists who fear that multicultural education will transform America in ways that will result in their own disempowerment. Ironically, the successes that multicultural education has experienced during the last decade have played a major role in provoking the attacks.[10]

For Banks, this debate over "American identity" will determine whether we achieve "racial peace" and "national salvation."[11]

Those whom Banks refers to as posing the dangerous threat to our educational system are a group of well-known educators and writers who have expressed concerns about multicultural education. In 1987, two books that dealt with the content of the curriculums used in our schools became surprise best-sellers and ignited a new debate about multicultural education. Allan Bloom, a professor of Social Thought at the University of Chicago, although primarily concerned about college curriculums, wrote a widely read book titled *The Closing of the American Mind*. He and E. D. Hirsch, in his book *Cultural Literacy*, claimed that schools and colleges were failing to pass on a core of common information and values that are fundamental if we are to survive as a unified society. For Hirsch at least, there was an immediate need to agree upon a "core curriculum" for all American children. He calls for a "return to a system of education that teaches all citizens an established vocabulary of culture, so that we can talk together using the same system of cultural referents."[12] Hirsch in his book refers to students who believe that Toronto is a city in Italy and another student who identifies an epic poem by Homer as the "Alamo." In response to the lack of basic knowledge, Hirsch and his colleagues have developed and implemented in a number of schools a "core curriculum which has been created to provide a common knowledge which is required in our society." Among other materials that have been produced is a list of 5,000 things, names, proverbs, quotes, and concepts that "literate Americans should know."[13] Critics would claim that the vast majority of these facts would be most helpful in a game of trivial pursuit. Even though not everyone agrees with this approach, Allan Bloom has been successful in spreading the idea that we need a common curriculum that is expressed today with the term "learning standards." Coupled with the perceived need for common standards or curriculum objectives are the concepts of high-stakes testing and accountability. Although the standards movement was called for in the *A Nation at Risk* report in 1983 and implemented by the No Child Left Behind legislation in 2002, that law also refers to the need for integrating the concept of multicultural education.

Bloom is also very clear in stating his belief in the importance of being specific about what should be taught.

> Instead of vague outcomes such as "First graders will be introduced to map skills," the geography section of the *Core Knowledge Sequence* specifies that first graders will learn the meaning of "east," "west," "north," and "south" and locate on a map the equator, the Atlantic and Pacific Oceans, the seven continents, the United States, Mexico, Canada, and Central America.[14]

It should be noted that even though he vehemently supports the inclusion of a specific core curriculum, it would still only constitute about 50 percent of the total school curriculum. Even with Bloom's approach, school districts and classroom teachers would have considerable flexibility in determining what occurs in our nation's classrooms. Unfortunately perhaps, the imposition of mandatory testing in language arts and math may restrict teachers' efforts to include multicultural projects. Teachers who are overly concerned about preparing students for tests are not likely to stray frequently into areas that will not appear on an examination. Still, Bloom and others would support high-stakes examinations and a fairly fixed curriculum because they believe that this has been a major factor in the success of students in nations such as Japan, Sweden, and France. The lack of curriculum coherence in the United States has been a source of criticism for many years. These individuals believe that "to achieve excellence and fairness for all," schools "must follow a coherent sequence of solid, specific content."[15]

Core curriculum advocates have spawned their own critics, who ask, "Who is going to decide what should be in the core curriculum?" They question whether it will be Hirsch and Bloom and other conservative intellectuals who will decide whether the curricular canons will again be Eurocentric, exclusionary, and dominated by white males.[16] Even more damning is the charge that

> much of the Hirsch/Bloom world view is outdated. Most Americans are now aware of the contributions of repressed cultures, more alert to how history has been rewritten and molded to the vision of the majority population, and accustomed to the notion that culture, like language, changes, and that we ought to be sensitive to those changes. Though Hirsch is right, as far as he goes, in his list of 5,000 things that savvy folk ought to know, he doesn't go far or deep enough. We need to know much more.[17]

At this point in the discussion, it could be instructive to consider what Horace Mann and the other founders of the public school movement might have thought about multicultural education. Mann's writing makes it clear that he was seeking to create schools where all children could develop common values "despite differences of class, creed, and national origin."[18] Mann wrote in the *Common School Journal* in 1839:

> I want to see the rich and the poor sit down side by side on equal terms, as members of one family—a great brotherhood—deeming no one distinguished above the rest but the best scholar and the best boy—giving free and natural play to their affections, at a time of life when lasting friendships are often formed, and worldliness and pride, and envy have not alienated heart from heart.[19]

One can conclude that even if Horace Mann did not support a complete core curriculum, he did insist on the teaching of common values. Unlike the Jacksonian Democrats during his lifetime, he saw these values as being agreed upon and enforced at the state level. The Whig Party was worried that Jacksonian democracy would create a "mobocracy" that would mean local rule by the "uneducated, unlettered, ignorant frontiersman and immigrants . . . [C]ommon school advocates saw public education as an agency for personal and societal moral regeneration."[20] In this respect, Horace Mann agreed with E. D. Hirsch that those who would benefit most from a common education were the poor. He might also conclude that the public school "would be a cultural agency that transmitted the U.S. cultural heritage to young people through literature and history."[21] On the other hand, although his goal was to cultivate a general political consciousness, Mann believed strongly that schools should not indoctrinate students in any single partisan political ideology.

It would seem that if faced with a choice between the analogies of schools as a "melting pot" or as a "salad bowl," Horace Mann would have chosen the melting pot, as it would more effectively assimilate diverse students into American citizens. Still, as a liberal, it would be hard to imagine him opposing the inclusion in the curriculum of information about the contributions of all groups in our nation's population. Whether he would think that the celebration of Black History Month was helpful or divisive, one can only guess. Because of his ongoing interest in how children learn, it would be fair to say that he would be studying carefully the research dealing with varied cultural learning styles. Finally, although he would most likely support the programs that seek to bring about assimilation and cultural literacy, his sincere concern for less fortunate children might well open his mind to the ideas of the multiculturalists. Along with multicultural education, another approach to education designed to improve the academic success of our children is the phenomenon we have labeled "school choice."

NOTES

1. Joel Spring, *The American School: 1642–2004* (Boston: McGraw-Hill, 2004), 3.

2. L. Dean Webb, Arlene Metha, and K. Forbis Jordan, *Foundations of American Education* (Upper Saddle River, NJ: Merrill, 2000), 277.

3. Webb, Metha, and Jordan, *Foundations*, 276.

4. "Multicultural Education in America," www.cyberessays.com/Politics/11.htm (accessed 4 November 2004), 2.

5. Myra Pollack Sadker and David Miller Sadker, *Teachers, Schools, and Society*, 5th ed. (Boston: McGraw-Hill, 2000), 96–97.

6. Sadker and Sadker, *Teachers, Schools, and Society*, 97.

7. Kevin Ryan and James M. Cooper, *Those Who Can, Teach* (Boston: Houghton Mifflin Company, 1995), 447.

8. Ryan and Cooper, *Those Who Can, Teach*, 447.

9. James A. Banks, "Multicultural Education: Development, Dimensions, and Challenges," *ENC Online*, www.enc.org/features/focus/archive/multi/document.shtm?input=ACQ-111511-1511 (accessed 20 September 2004), 2.

10. Banks, "Multicultural Education," 15.

11. Banks, "Multicultural Education," 15.

12. Rick Simonson and Scott Walker, eds., *Multi-cultural Literacy* (St. Paul, MN: Graywolf Press, 1988), ix.

13. Simonson and Walker, *Multi-cultural Literacy*, ix.

14. Don Kauchak, Paul Eggen, and Mary D. Burbank, *Charting a Professional Course: Issues and Controversies in Education* (Upper Saddle River, NJ: Merrill Prentice Hall, 2005), 91–92.

15. Kauchak, Eggen, and Burbank, *Charting*, 94.

16. Sadker and Sadker, *Teachers, Schools, and Society*, 257.

17. Simonson and Walker, *Multi-cultural Literacy*, x–xi.

18. V. T. Thayer, *Formative Ideas in American Education* (New York: Dodd, Mead and Company, Inc., 1974), 96.

19. Thayer, *Formative Ideas*, 97.

20. Gerald L. Guteck, *Historical and Philosophical Foundations of Education* (Upper Saddle River, NJ: Merrill Prentice Hall, 2005), 218–19.

21. Guteck, *Foundations*, 226.

10

THE CHOICE ISSUE

It is interesting that there are thirteen schools of choice in the state of Massachusetts called the Horace Mann Charter Schools.[1] One can only speculate what the father of the common school movement would think about his name being used for this new type of public school. Charter schools are just one of the ways that our society has developed to give parents and students the opportunity to select their school from a number of choices.

Although we have always had private schools that have offered alternatives to tax-supported schools, attendance at such schools in the past was limited to those who could afford to pay tuition. The current movement toward school choice seeks to allow parents to choose options other than their neighborhood school and in some cases, nonpublic schools. Many trace the beginning of the current choice movement to the writings of the economist Milton Friedman. A half century ago, Friedman proposed a voucher system that would give to parents a voucher worth a specified amount of money to allow their children to attend either a public or a private school.[2] The argument for this system and for the idea of school choice generally is very much in keeping with the American fondness for a competitive free market economic system. Proponents of school choice have argued that because they are free, public schools have a virtual monopoly on education in the United States. Because of the certainty that there will always be customers, public schools have not been adequately motivated to improve their product. Critics suggest that they have become inefficient bureaucracies that are burdened by unnecessary federal, state, and local regulations. The result is, according to the critics, that our tax-supported schools are poorly managed institutions where creativity and innovation are extremely difficult.

Others would place at least part of the blame on administrative and teacher unions, both of which critics suggest have vested interest in the status quo. Along with the need for change in public schools, supporters of choice argue that when parents and students are allowed to choose their schools, there is more likely to be a family commitment to that school. In addition, it has been suggested that the competition created by any choice option will cause the current public schools to improve in order to ensure their survival. Whether it is through a voucher plan, charter schools, magnet schools, or an open enrollment system, advocates of school choice are convinced that students will benefit. These arguments have appealed to many in our society.

The first movement toward school choice took place in large school districts with the establishment of magnet schools in many of our cities. Most often, these schools have been high schools, and each of them has initiated a specific academic focus for its program. A city board of education might create a school for the arts, a vocational school, one for bilingual students, or perhaps an honors high school for highly talented, college-bound students. At the same time, most larger cities that have experimented with magnet schools have also maintained a number of comprehensive neighborhood high schools for those students who are not interested in one of the magnet schools.

The magnet schools are public schools under the control of the local board of education. Their students are required to meet all of the national, state, and local curriculum and testing requirements. At the same time, the local board includes provisions for special opportunities in the area of the magnet school's focus. For instance, a high school for the arts has additional opportunities for music and art. This might include elective courses in music theory and competition along with a variety of performing groups. Art students in such a school have the opportunity to take electives in art history, as well as in hands-on courses such as ceramics and sculpture. While some magnet schools might accept most or all of the applicants, those created for art, music, or honors students have additional requirements. Any child wishing to attend a school for the arts might have to submit a portfolio of artwork while a music student would be required to have an audition. Honors students are most often chosen based on grade point average, teacher recommendations, or perhaps an entrance examination.

The possibility of giving students and parents a choice was only one of the motivations for establishing magnet schools. Perhaps even more important for many urban boards of education was the goal of breaking down the neighborhood basis for assigning students to a school. This became a popular cause in the decade of the sixties because so many urban neighborhoods had become segregated. As noted earlier, "white flight" to the suburbs had created neighborhood schools that were made up primarily of minority students. The hope was by offering a choice of schools, students would leave their segregated neighborhoods to attend a school that had a more diverse population.[3] Given the current status of racial segregation in our urban schools, it is not clear that magnet schools have made a significant difference in the racial balance in most urban schools. Finally, those who championed the magnet school concept undoubtedly hoped that by creating some outstanding schools in their city, white parents would be less likely to flee to the suburbs. At the beginning of the twenty-first century, magnet schools were located in thirty-three states. Still, magnet schools are not without their critics. Those who have reservations about this choice initiative have raised questions such as the following:

- How have magnet schools affected the comprehensive schools in the district? If additional funds were spent in a high school for the arts on musical instruments or art supplies, might this not reduce expenditures for the comprehensive, nonmagnet high schools?

- Have magnet schools drained off the most talented and academically able students? Would this leave more discipline problems in the comprehensive schools and perhaps dilute the academic programs for students attending neighborhood, nonmagnet high schools? Would these schools be left with students who have discipline and truancy problems, as well as those who need special education?
- How would the district solve the problem of transportation? Would the taxpayers provide additional dollars to help students attend the school of their choice? The other option would be to make it the parents' responsibility to provide transportation. If this is done, might the cost make it impossible for some parents to pay to transport their child across the city?

Whether one supports the idea of magnet schools, it is true that in most cities, they do have significant political support. As a result, it is likely that this form of choice will not disappear in the near future.

Along with magnet schools a number of districts are attempting an open enrollment approach. Under such a plan, the requirement that children attend a neighborhood school is lifted at least for some students. If a district has five elementary schools, a family could at least apply to a school other than their neighborhood school. The right to attend a different public school in the district is not absolute in that neighborhood families are often given the first choice if they wish to attend the school closest to their home. Because of this opportunity, a popular school might have only a limited number of vacancies for students, even though hundreds of students from outside the neighborhood might apply. An open enrollment plan can positively affect segregation within a district, and it does create motivation for all schools to seek to hold their students. It is also true that such a system can be instituted in smaller districts that could have several elementary schools, even though they each have only one or two high schools.

Abandoning the neighborhood concept for an open enrollment plan can also create problems. Very popular schools could eventually have more than their share of the best and brightest students. Unfortunately, this can also happen with teachers in both open enrollment systems and magnet schools. If teacher contracts require that all teaching vacancies in the district be posted to allow teachers to transfer to other schools within the district, the schools with the best reputations will draw applications from many district faculty. The elementary schools in the more affluent and safer neighborhoods might draw a considerable number of experienced teachers. At the same time, a magnet school specializing in science or the arts would be an attractive option for teachers who are well qualified in their fields. Open enrollment policies also create the same transportation problem as magnet schools. In any case, the open enrollment option does not impact some districts dramatically. For instance, in the fall of 2004, when the Washington, D.C., district created such a system, only 106 out of over 25,000 eligible students even applied to leave their neighborhood school. Of this number, only 68 were accepted for transfer. This plan will undoubtedly involve more students in the future, but the poor initial response surprised and disappointed local officials.[4] While the practice of establishing open enrollment and magnet schools has occurred in many large districts, there are two other types of educational choice options that may be expanding even more rapidly.

Many parents in districts of every size are choosing to homeschool their children. Two decades ago, it was estimated that approximately 12,500 students in the United States were being homeschooled. Today the number is somewhere between 1 million and 1.5 million students. Parents are making the choice to teach their own children for a number of reasons. There are certainly fears in some areas about the safety of public schools. For others, it is a lack of academic rigor in the public schools that motivates parents. The largest group choosing this option are those who are seeking to impart their own religious values to their children. For these primarily Protestant parents, the public schools have ceased to teach true Christian values. The fact that home schooling allows parents to teach one-on-one to their children perhaps helps to explain why these students score between the sixty-fifth and ninetieth percentile on standardized tests.[5]

Unfortunately, there are a minority of homeschooled students who might have achieved more academically in a school setting. Critics of the practice argue that many homeschooled children are deprived of the experience of meeting and associating with a diverse group of peers and that this is a disadvantage to them as they move into a college or university. Because all parents, even those with a limited educational background, are allowed to teach their children at home, some rely on a packaged curriculum that is published in some cases by religious organizations. Such curriculums may have a narrow focus, especially in fields such as science. Other homeschool parents rely heavily on computer programs, especially for students at the high school level. Perhaps the most significant problem with homeschooling high school students is the lack of content background of some parents in subjects such as chemistry, physics, and advanced math.

There are other potential difficulties when one chooses to teach his or her child at home. Even though homeschool parents have banded together to provide social activities and specialized academic programs for their children, many homeschooled children mix socially primarily with children from families like their own. Also, because schools in most states are not required to allow these children to participate in extracurricular activities in their neighborhood school, homeschooled students are often denied the opportunity to take part in student councils or plays, or to work on the school newspaper or yearbook. Despite the growing popularity of homeschooling, it is not likely to put the public schools out of business. Since so many mothers and fathers both hold down full-time jobs, homeschooling is not a realistic option for most families. Still, we cannot ignore the fact that a significant number of parents are choosing not to enroll their children in the public schools.

The fastest-growing choice option today is the creation of charter schools. Currently, thirty-eight states allow the formation of such schools, and the number continues to grow. Although there is no definitive statistic, it has been estimated that there are now at least 2,500 such schools.[6] Laws involving charter schools vary somewhat from state to state. In most cases, the process begins when the state legislature and the governor approve legislation allowing for the formation of a limited number of such schools in the state. Application forms are made available to anyone wishing to begin a charter school. Initially, charter schools were proposed by the former president of the American Federation of Teachers, Albert Shanker, in a speech in 1988. At that time, Shanker was theorizing that the primary founders of such schools would be teachers who worked in the public school system. The hope was that the charter schools would allow creative and ambitious teachers to escape much of the state and district bureaucracy and create innovative programs that would better meet the needs of the students. As the concept has expanded, a variety of individuals and groups have been successful in gaining charters. More recently, a new entry into the movement has been for-profit corporations such as the Edison Project, which have successfully gained charters in a number of states. For them, the automatic funding from the state and local district has all but insured that charter schools can be a profitable investment for their stockholders.

The first state to try out this new concept was Minnesota in 1991. In Minnesota and most states, a successful application to open a charter school must have the approval of both a state agency and the local board of education where the school will be located. Applications are judged on questions such as the following:

- What is the curriculum going to be at each grade level?
- What means of assessment will be used to judge the effectiveness of the curriculum?
- What are the arrangements for housing the new school?
- How will the school utilize parent involvement? Most states require the formation of a special committee made up of parents and school personnel to help govern the school, even though the ultimate responsibility remains with the local board of education of the district where the charter school is established.
- What qualifications will be used when hiring administrators, teachers, and staff? Many of the laws allowing the creation of charter schools permit waiving the requirement for teacher certification, at least for a specified percentage of the faculty.

It should be noted that although charter schools are given freedom from most state and local regulations, the schools cannot be sponsored by religious denominations. All of the church-and-state requirements governing other public schools are also applicable to charter schools. Realistically, a charter is merely a contract between the founders of the school and the school district and state. This contract usually covers a specific length of time that the school will be given to meet its established educational objectives. At the close of this period, the charter school must reapply to continue to remain in operation. There are also frequently provisions that allow the local school board or the state education department to close the school during the course of the contract. There have been a number of examples of schools that have been closed or have failed to be rechartered. Some critics have charged that these schools are insufficiently supervised. In Texas in 2001 ten charter schools were closed and their students forced to repeat a grade because of poor record-keeping. The National Education Association has also publicized the fact that test scores for charter schools in Texas were, in 2001, lower than those of the public schools in the state.[7]

In Arizona, a school was closed because it was secretly teaching religion, while in the District of Columbia, the charters of three of its seventeen charter schools were revoked. Problems have also arisen in California, Minnesota, Wisconsin, and Pennsylvania.[8] By far, the biggest problem has been in California, where sixty "mostly storefront" schools went out of business. Still, it should be noted that given the fact that there are over five hundred such schools in California, the closing of sixty is not as dramatic as it might seem.[9]

Even though there have been some problems, charter schools remain a popular option, especially in cities. Recently the idea has gained support among many minority parents who continue to see their children falling behind academically in the regular public schools. A number of city mayors, especially those who have some power in the management of schools, are pushing the idea with their constituents.[10]

Some urban public schools are also experimenting with other types of school choice. *Education Week* recently published an article describing the growing number of single-sex public schools. There are now thirty-four such programs in public school systems and a total of 113 schools that offer single-sex classes. Such schools have long been an option if a family could afford to send its child to a private single-sex school, but now the same choice is available in some public school systems.[11]

Even more controversial than single-sex public schools is the voucher plan that actually started the discussions on school choice over a half century ago. Although there are several ways to implement voucher programs, the current approaches could be described as follows:

Universal Vouchers
> Allowing all parents to direct funds set aside for education by the government for their children to a school of their choice, whether the school is public, private, or religious, and in effect, separating the government financing of education from the government operation of schools.

Means-tested Vouchers
> Enabling income-eligible families, usually in limited numbers, to direct funds set aside for education by the government to pay for tuition at the public, private, or religious school of their choice.
> *Examples:* Cleveland, Milwaukee

Failing Schools Vouchers
> Allowing all parents whose children attend public schools identified as failing to direct funds set aside for education by the government to a better-performing public, private, or religious school of their choice. There are no income requirements, and eligibility is based solely on the success of individual public schools.
> *Example:* Florida[12]

A very significant difference between most voucher plans and the other forms of school choice is that some of these plans allow public money to be given to schools sponsored by a religious denomination.

This of course raises the question of whether such funding is a violation of the First Amendment to the federal Constitution, which states that "Congress shall make no law respecting an establishment of religion."[13]

There have been a number of cases related to this issue. For example, the Florida state courts have on three occasions declared the Florida voucher plans of their state unconstitutional because they allow "students to attend religious schools with taxpayer money." Governor Jeb Bush plans to appeal these decisions to the Florida Supreme Court. On the other hand, the Florida Teachers Union applauded the decisions.[14] In Maine, where the state pays tuition for some students to attend private schools, a federal appeals court ruled recently that the state was "not required to pay tuition for children attending religious schools."[15]

There have also been state court decisions that have supported the use of public funds for religious schools. Ultimately, this issue is likely to end in the national Supreme Court. Since the Republican Party has long supported school choice, including the use of vouchers for religious schools, the Republican victory in the national election in 2004 could lead to the appointment of judges at every level of the federal court system who will be comfortable with the use of tax dollars to finance religious schools. This being the case, it is possible that school vouchers for religious schools could be ruled constitutional in the immediate future.

This, however, will not occur without a fight. Along with public school teachers and administrators, as well as most boards of education, there are other opponents of the implementation of vouchers in education. The arguments most often used in opposing such plans are:

- Any plan to give students a choice of schools can create transportation problems for either the parents or the district.
- Under a voucher system, both public and private schools might spend significant amounts of money on advertising and recruiting. Neither of these activities results in improvements in the academic program.

- Because the most prestigious private schools would cost much more than any voucher, poor families still could not afford the most expensive private schools.
- Many wealthy parents who can afford the high tuition cost of some private schools would receive an unneeded government subsidy.
- Public schools would have to accept all students while private schools could be more selective. As a result, special education students and children with discipline problems would end up in the public schools, thus making them a "dumping ground" for difficult students.

Voters in seven states have unanimously turned down voucher plans in the years between 1972 and 2000.[16] More recently, though, support has been growing, especially in cities and among minority populations. There is no question that there will continue to be proposals for new voucher plans, charter schools, and open enrollment options. Before turning to the possible position of Horace Mann on this important movement, it would be instructive to examine briefly some of the data that have been gathered on the effectiveness of certain "choice" programs. First, it must be pointed out that we have not even come close to establishing a national voucher system and that all of the choice options are governed by state law and local policies. The choice programs that have evolved range from schools that are liberal and experimental to those that truly attempt to go "back to the basics."

It is understandable that we have yet to have definitive studies on the success of these alternatives on a national scale. Research done on the Milwaukee voucher program funded by a school choice group in Wisconsin was reported as evidence that bolstered the case for tuition vouchers. A *Washington Post* article describing the study also quoted independent experts who raised questions about the validity of the research.[17]

On the negative side, a study by the Federal Department of Education concluded that an

analysis of test scores from 2003 shows that children in charter schools generally did not perform as well on exams as those in regular public schools. The analysis . . . largely confirms an earlier report on the same statistics by the American Federation of Teachers.[18]

In the same *New York Times* article, Jeanne Allen, president of the Center for Educational Reform, which supports charters, stated that "studies . . . purport to show stronger results for charters in comparisons that are statewide, rather than national." She goes on to claim that "charter school students in the aggregate are in a dead heat with students in regular schools."[19]

Despite clear-cut evidence of their ineffectiveness, choice programs have many important supporters. They include George W. Bush, who has been quoted as saying, "I support school choice. If the neighborhood school is failing in its basic mission, parents and teachers don't need more excuses. They need answers. . . . A parent with options is a parent with influence."[20] It would appear that he is not alone, and it may well be that there are a growing number of federal and state legislators as well as judges who agree with the president.

Despite the current popularity of school choice, there are also a large number of outspoken opponents. In a book titled *Schools for Sale* and subtitled *Why Free Market Policies Won't Improve America's Schools, and What Will*, Ernest R. House argues that schools are different than businesses and that competition will not improve education.[21]

I believe that Horace Mann too would have had major concerns about some of the current school choice initiatives in the United States. His vision for the common school was that all children, at least in their first eight years of education, would have a common curriculum that would include specific lessons in what we now call values education and citizenship. The schools would include children who were rich and poor and of every race and creed. Although he did not talk about eliminating private schools, he sought to make the common school as good as or better than the best private schools. Of all the choice plans, I believe he would be most opposed to a voucher plan that allows public money to be spent for denominational schools. Although he would applaud the innovation hoped for in the charter school movement, I believe that he would have preferred to see the traditional neighborhood public schools utilize the best ideas available, thus making charter schools unnecessary.

For a man whose adult life was devoted to the promotion of public schools, I expect he would have agreed with these words from the book *The American Dream and the Public Schools:*

> On vouchers, then, both politics and substance lead to the same conclusion: large-scale privatization of public schooling would not necessarily promote individual success, and would undermine the public's long-standing commitment to put the American dream into practice through the shared institution of the schools. Americans believe strongly in what Terry Moe describes as the public school ideology.
>
> Many Americans simply like the idea of a public school system. They see it as an expression of local democracy and a pillar of the local community; they admire the egalitarian principles on which it is based, they think it deserves our commitment and support, and they tend to regard as subversive any notion that private schools should play a larger role in educating the nation's children.
>
> In our terms, Americans believe that schools should not only promote the ability of individuals to pursue their dreams but should be the vehicle for Americans to learn to engage in a common enterprise of shared citizenship. Voucher programs for private and parochial schools violate this ideology. Americans love the idea of choices. But school choice is too weak a lever to provide the answer to the problems of American education. Help can only come on the difficult roads of finance equity, school reform, and inclusion.[22]

While choice is an area that might have bothered Horace Mann, there are other innovations in our classrooms during recent years that he might have felt more comfortable with. We will now consider the issue of technology and attempt to determine whether its use in the classroom would fit in the original vision that established our public schools.

NOTES

1. Massachusetts Department of Education, "Information about Horace Mann Charter Schools," www.doe.mass.edu/charter/horacemann.html (accessed 14 September 2004), 1.

2. Myra Pollack Sadker and David Miller Sadker, *Teachers, Schools, and Society*, 5th ed. (Boston: McGraw-Hill, 2000), 152.

3. Education Commission of the States, "Magnet Schools: Pros and Cons," 2004, www.ecs.org/html/IssueSection.asp?issueid=80&s=Quick +Facts (accessed 7 March 2004), 1.

4. Sewell Chan, "Few D.C. Students Transfer Schools," *Washington Post*, 10 October 2004, www.washingtonpost.com/wp-dyn/articles/A20821-2004Oct9.html (accessed 15 October 2004), 1.

5. Myra Pollack Sadker and David Miller Sadker, *Teachers, Schools, and Society*, 6th ed. (Boston: McGraw-Hill, 2003), 166–67.

6. Alan Richard, "The State of Charter Schools Nationwide," *Education Week*, 20 March 2002, www.iedx.org/article_1asp?ConentID=EN520&Sec tionGroupID=NEWS (accessed 7 March 2004).

7. National Education Association, "Charter Schools," www.nea.org/ charter/ (accessed 14 September 2004), 2.

8. National Education Association, "Charter Schools," 3.

9. Sam Dillon, "Collapse of 60 Charter Schools Leaves Californians Scrambling," *New York Times*, 17 September 2004, www.nytimes.com/2004/ 0917/education/17charter.html?hp (accessed 17 September 2004), 1.

10. Caroline Hendrie, "City Mayors Turn to Charter Schools," *Education Week*, 27 October 2004, www.edweek.org/ew/articles/2004/10/27/09may ors.h24.html (accessed 27 October 2004), 1.

11. Tal Barak, "Number of Single-Sex Schools Growing," *Education Week*, 20 October 2004, www.edweek.org/ew/articles/2004/10/20/08ocr-s1.h24 .html, 1 (accessed 3 November 2003).

12. Milton & Rose D. Friedman Foundation, "Vouchers," www.fried manfoundation.org/schoolchoice/index.html (accessed 7 March 2004), 1.

13. Nathaniel Platt and Muriel Jane Drummond, *Our Nation From its Creation* (Englewood Cliffs, NJ: Prentice-Hall, Inc., 1964), xxviii.

14. Joetta L. Sack, "Florida Vouchers Dealt Another Legal Blow," *Education Week*, 24 November 2004, www.edweek.org/ew/articles/2004/11/24/ 13fla.h24.html (accessed 28 November 2004), 1.

15. Joetta L. Sack, "Court: Maine Aid Program Can Bar Religious Schools," *Education Week*, 3 November 2004, www.edweek.org/ew/articles/ 2004/11/03/10maine.h24.html (accessed 28 November 2004), 1.

16. National Education Association, "Voters Recently Reject Vouchers," www.nes.org/vouchers/vouchervotes.html (accessed 11 March 2004), 1.

17. Sewell Chan, "Study Bolsters Case for Tuition Vouchers," *Washington Post*, 29 September 2004, www.washingtonpost.com/wp-dyn/articles/ A58082-2004Sep28.html (accessed 20 September 2004), 1.

18. Diana Jean Schemo, "A Second Report Shows Charter School Students Not Performing as Well as Other Students," *New York Times*, 16 December 2004, www.nytimes.com/2004/12/16/education16charter.html (accessed 16 December 2004), 1.

19. Schemo, "Second Report," 2.

20. Jennifer Hochschild and Nathan Scovronick, *The American Dream and the Public Schools* (Oxford: Oxford University Press, 2003), 107.

21. Ernest R. House, *Schools for Sale: Why Free Market Policies Won't Improve America's Schools, and What Will* (New York: Teachers College Press, 1998), 1–3.

22. Hochschild and Scovronick, *American Dream*, 132.

11

THE TECHNOLOGY

During the past half century, school districts in the United States have spent billions of dollars on technology designed to enhance student learning. Beginning with slide, filmstrip, and movie projectors, we have seen the introduction of ditto machines, educational television, VCRs, color copiers, and computers. Each of these machines has been purchased to help teachers do their job more effectively. As a society, we accepted the premise that the introduction of this technology would make a positive difference in student learning. Especially with computers, public support for new technology for our classrooms and libraries has been overwhelming. In large part, this was because parents and other voters were personally experiencing in their workplace the importance of the computer revolution.

Before computers, the first major technological initiative in our schools was educational television. Few questioned the positive impact of programs such as *Sesame Street* and *Mr. Rogers*. More recently, supporters of educational television have pointed to the benefits of cable channels such as the History Channel and the Discovery Channel. At the same time, many others now point to the negative effects of children watching too much of what is available on television. Critics such as Diane Ravitch have suggested that many parents have surrendered much of their responsibility, and that too many children are learning how to behave from television.[1]

Other writers have suggested that the fact that young people spend so much of their time watching television, and now playing fast-paced computer games, has made the teachers' job more difficult. Making classes exciting enough to maintain the shrinking attention span of their students has become a new challenge for teachers. It is not surprising that many instructors have chosen to intersperse frequent videos and clever PowerPoint presentations into their lessons.

Although there is little question that watching television outside of the classroom has had its effect on children, it is not as clear that television used in the classroom has made a significant difference in student learning. Approximately 10,000 schools have accepted an offer of free television equipment, including a satellite dish, in exchange for allowing a private company to broadcast into each classroom a ten-minute newscast. Along with the news each day, the students also receive two minutes of commercials. By the year 2000, 25 percent of the secondary schools in the United States had Channel One broadcasts piped into their classrooms.[2] Many would question the value of such a trade-off.

In the late '60s and early '70s, a large number of schools purchased television sets for each of their classrooms in the expectation that they would be able to supplement traditional instruction with programs developed by the public television network. Videotape recorders were made available to teachers during the next two decades. Today, the technology in our more advanced classrooms allows teachers to, on the same piece of equipment, play DVDs, present PowerPoint presentations, and have immediate Internet access. The computer has replaced the television set as the primary source of educational technology. It is not unusual to find, even in an elementary classroom, as many as five computers for student use as well as a more sophisticated system for the teacher.

Most young people like to work on computers. Some students who are reluctant to write a composition by hand are more willing to if they can use a word processor. Also, to many young people, practicing math problems on the computer is preferable to the traditional methods used in math class. The speed and vastness of the Internet for information-gathering and research cannot be denied.

Certainly learning keyboarding and other computer skills appears to be essential in a world where computers are an integral tool in almost every workplace. Online learning programs also offer opportunities that cannot occur in some schools. Therefore, it is difficult to criticize a technology that allows a student in a remote high school to take a calculus course online from a top-notch professor at a far-off university. As a nation engaged in a technological global economy, we cannot afford to graduate students from our high schools who are not prepared to either move directly into the workplace or attend an institution of higher learning, both of which require a degree of competence in the use of computers.

There are also a number of studies that have shown positive results from using technology to improve student learning. For instance, there was a study in West Virginia in 1999 that concluded that "technology-enhanced" students "achieved significantly higher scores on standardized basic knowledge tests in several grades than those without enhancement." A thirteen-year study completed by the Apple Classroom of Tomorrow found that "introduction of technology into classrooms can significantly increase the potential for learning, especially in collaboration, information access, and expression and representation of student's thoughts and ideas."[3]

The influence of the computer in our schools can already be felt, as seen by these statistics gathered by the Pew Research Center in 2002. This report noted that:

94 percent of students use the Internet for school research;
71 percent used it as a major source for their most recent school project;
58 percent have used a Web site set up by their school or class;
34 percent have downloaded study aids; and
17 percent have created a Web page related to a school project.[4]

Not everyone agrees that technology has a significant positive effect on public education. In regard to television viewing in the classroom, "critics charge that watching television is an unproductive use of class time, an activity that at best should be used as an instructional supplement to be viewed at home or in the school's media re-source room."[5] Other educators question whether students should be spending significant amounts of class time working on a computer.

William D. Pflaum, in a book titled *The Technology Fix: The Promise and Reality of Computers in Our Schools*, cites his year-long study from which he concluded "technology's bold promises have been broken." He identified the original arguments supporting the use of comput-ers in schools as follows:

- Schools would create student-centered classrooms, where com-puters that tailored instruction to the individual needs of every learner would replace the teacher-centered classroom.
- Students would no longer be passive recipients of information. Technology would empower them to become active partici-pants in the construction of their own knowledge. With access to the world's ever-expanding pool of knowledge, the class-room would become the world.
- Skills would not be neglected. Engaging multimedia programs would adapt to each student's learning style. Static textbooks would gather dust, replaced by dynamic, always-up-to-date learning resources.
- Computer technology would revolutionize the classroom struc-ture. Teachers would learn alongside their students. They would be facilitators of student-learning, not purveyors of a one-size-fits-all curriculum. Test scores would soar or test scores would disappear altogether.[6]

That we have so far fallen short of these lofty goals seems indisputable.

Other critics have pointed to a reality that has been labeled the "digital divide." One study conducted by the Corporation for Public Broadcasting found that in 2003, 66 percent of high-income children had Internet access at home while only 29 percent of the lower-income children had a home computer.[7] One can guess that this dif-ference has only become greater. It is also very likely that the schools attended by less affluent children, especially those in rural areas and in some cities, have fewer computers available in their schools than schools in affluent suburban districts. The lack of access to computers for research papers and other purposes can only be another disadvantage for poor children.

It has also been pointed out that schools have made serious errors in their haste to bring computers into every classroom. Some districts have failed to make long-range plans for how they were going to integrate the use of computers into their curriculum. This, coupled with the lack of in-depth training for faculty, has resulted in far too many computers being underused in our nation's classrooms. Districts also may have underestimated the cost of maintaining their equipment. Those that have not provided sufficient support often have found that equipment could not be kept in good repair. Other schools spent so much on the hardware, they had little left to purchase the necessary educational software. Finally, some districts failed to consider the rapid obsolescence of their equipment. While initial expenditures for providing Internet services and hardware might have been provided by a special bond issue, keeping the system current requires significant outlays in the annual budget. Even the strongest supporters of the use of computers in schools would admit that most school districts have thus far failed to fully utilize the technology they have invested in.

At the same time, a whole new industry is emerging that allows students in the public schools as well as those at the college level to take not only single courses but complete degree programs online. A Web site (www.directdegree.com) lists online degree programs at all levels. Included are high school, undergraduate, and graduate degrees in areas such as the liberal arts, education and teaching, and business administration. These degrees are offered by some colleges as well as by numerous for-profit companies.[8] Needless to say, there are those who question the validity of such programs. For example, teacher educators might take issue with allowing a student to complete a degree in teacher education without having had the experience of observing and participating in classes that instruct students on teaching methods. They would also see as a great deficiency the lack of experience online students would have in actually teaching lessons. People studying business administration could certainly benefit from participating in face-to-face discussions and simulations. Science instructors might also suggest that computer lab experiments are not nearly as valuable as a hands-on approach in an actual science laboratory.

The federal government has become involved in attempting to identify educational programs that the popular press has labeled "diploma mills." A CNN report claims that "most often" these "phony degrees" are offered online. In testimony before Congress, one critic of these programs claimed that there are more than two hundred of these "diploma mills" that gross over $200,000,000 per year. There currently is no law against such degree programs even though some go so far as to simply "sell degrees for a flat fee."[9]

Given the fact that the debate continues over this importance of technology in education, it would be interesting to speculate on how Horace Mann would feel about this important initiative in public education. There is no question that Mann believed very strongly in the absolute importance of having children exposed directly to teachers who would provide strong role models. In his own words, Mann wrote:

> To save a considerable portion of the rising generation from falling back into the condition of half-civilized or savage life, what other instrumentality does society afford than to send into every obscure and hidden district in the state a young man or a young woman whose education is sound; whose language is well-selected; whose pronunciation and tones of voice are correct and attractive; whose manners are gentle and refined; all of whose topics of conversation are elevating and instructive; whose benignity of heart is constantly manifested in acts of civility, courtesy and kindness; and who spreads a nameless charm over whatever circle may be entered. Such a person should the teacher of every common school be.[10]

Along with this almost impossible role description, Mann also stated that teachers must somehow create within their students an agreed-upon list of Christian virtues. A central theme in Mann's thinking about education "is the primacy of moral over intellectual education." It would seem hard for a teacher to impart these values and to be an extraordinary role model in an environment where students were spending most of their time on computers. To have a chance of accomplishing these noncognitive objectives it would seem that students would need to be involved individually and in groups with their teacher, discussing important philosophical issues and moral dilemmas.

Horace Mann also saw the need for the schools to create active and concerned citizens. The opening sentence in his ninth annual report to the Massachusetts Board of Education states that "one of the highest and most valuable objects, to which the influences of a school can be made conducive, consist in training our children to self-government."[11] This is another task that requires teachers to personally engage with students and to offer opportunities to solve problems collectively. Horace Mann believed that it is essential that teachers somehow pass on to their students much more than the knowledge of facts, but also certain qualities of heart and mind. In his own words, "If we do not develop their capacities, if we do not enrich their minds with knowledge, imbue their hearts with the love of truth and duty, and a reverence for all things sacred and holy, then our republic must go down to destruction."[12]

Despite the fact that Horace Mann continually emphasized the importance of the teacher as a role model, he also was unquestionably an innovator in regard to teaching methods. In his seventh annual report, he writes about what one author suggested are "some of the most familiar features of our present-day schools—the word method of teaching reading, oral instruction, elementary science, language exercises, geography built upon the life around, music and drawing."[13] None of these ideas or methods were prevalent in the schools during Mann's lifetime.

Joy Elmer Morgan states in her book *Horace Mann: His Ideas and Ideals*:

> Were Horace Mann alive today he would be considered the most progressive of educators. . . . It is evident that Horace Mann was scientifically minded on educational matters long before his time. . . . It is only the man of exceptional ability who has the power to set aside the instinctive aversion to change which all adults have and to consider a

novel action on its merits. Horace Mann had that power. . . . Perhaps there is no better tribute to his far-seeing genius than that the new era foreseen by him did not begin to materialize until two generations later.[14]

Others have written about Mann's tendency to support reform in the classroom. Historian Rush Welter has claimed that Horace Mann was "the country's leading pedagogical reformer."[15]

It is hard to believe that a man who is known as a "reformer," a "progressive," and a lover of science would not be open to the potential benefit of technology in our schools. It is unlikely that he would agree with online classes or degrees, which greatly restrict the personal contact with an outstanding teacher. Because of his strong commitment to the teacher as a personal role model and an instructor in transmitting Christian virtues and positive traits of citizenship, it would seem that any program that hindered the accomplishment of these objectives would not have been attractive to Horace Mann.

At the same time, this man who so respected science and a liberal approach to teaching could well have become excited by the potential of the Internet, the novelty of PowerPoint, and the ability to communicate easily with people throughout the world. Certainly the ability to project appropriate pictures, maps, and charts on a screen would be seen as a great advantage for any teacher. Still, it is not hard to conclude that Mann would be opposed to classrooms where students spent a significant amount of time sitting alone at a computer. For Horace Mann, technology would be a tool, but it would never be allowed to reduce the importance of the classroom teacher. It is to the teacher to which we now turn.

NOTES

1. Diane Ravitch, *Left Back* (New York: Simon and Schuster, 2000), 456.
2. Sarah Mondale and Sarah B. Patton, eds., *School* (Boston: Beacon Press), 202.

3. Jack L. Nelson, Stuart B. Palonsky, and Mary Rose McCarthy, *Critical Issues in Education: Dialogues and Dialectics* (Boston: McGraw-Hill, 2004), 326.

4. Nelson, Palonsky, and McCarthy, *Critical Issues*, 327.

5. Myra Pollack Sadker and David Miller Sadker, *Teachers, Schools, and Society*, 6th ed. (Boston: McGraw-Hill, 2003), 519.

6. William D. Pflaum, *The Technology Fix: The Promise and Reality of Computers in Our Schools*, (Alexandria, Va.: Association for Supervision and Curriculum Development, 2004), available at www.ascd.org/publications/books/104002/intro.html (accessed 4 March 2004), 2.

7. Allan C. Ornstein and Daniel U. Levine, *Foundations of Education* (Boston: Houghton Mifflin, 2006), 348.

8. www.directdegree.com.

9. CNN.com, "New methods used to expose diploma mills," 2 February 2005, http://www.cnn.com/2005/EDUCATION/02/02/bogus.degrees.ap/index.html (accessed 3 February 2005), 1.

10. Joy Elmer Morgan, *Horace Mann, His Ideas and Ideals* (Washington, DC: National Home Library Foundation, 1936), 134.

11. Lawrence A. Cremin, ed., *The Republic and the School: Horace Mann on the Education of Free Men* (New York: Bureau of Publications, Teachers College, Columbia University, 1957), 57.

12. Cremin, *Republic and the School*, 143.

13. Morgan, *Horace Mann, His Ideas and Ideals*, 26.

14. Morgan, *Horace Mann, His Ideas and Ideals*, 37–38.

15. Rush Welter, *Popular Education and Democratic Thought in America* (New York: Columbia University Press, 1962), 98.

12

THE TEACHERS

There is no question that for Horace Mann the most important factor in determining the success of a school was the effectiveness of the classroom teachers. Apparently, Americans today agree with this conclusion. Well-known educator John Goodlad recalls his own experience in addressing the significance of classroom teachers:

> Over the past year, I have been asking members of groups to which I speak to select from four items the one they believe to have the most promise for improving our schools. . . .
>   • Standards and tests mandated by all states;
>   • A qualified, competent teacher in every classroom;
>   • Non-promotion and grade retention for all students who fail to reach grade level standards on the tests;
>   • Schools of choice for all parents.
> From an audience of about one thousand people at the 2001 National School Boards Association Conference, one person chose the first. All the rest chose the second, which usually is the unanimous choice, whatever the group.[1]

Although it has always been central to the effectiveness of any school, historically, the teaching profession has evolved slowly through the centuries. Perhaps the first method for training teachers began in the Middle Ages as part of the guild system. A number of young men learned to be teachers by being apprenticed to a master teacher. It is interesting that today, many schools have adopted such a system as part of the training of new teachers. Many districts now have teacher mentor programs for their newest faculty members. An experienced teacher is assigned to help a newcomer during the first several years of his or her career.

Formal classroom training for teachers began in England as early as 1438 at Cambridge University, where a teacher-training institution was established. The curriculum included classes in teaching methods as well as a student teaching experience.[2]

The training of teachers was not a major consideration in colonial America. In the New England colonies, schools were established at the local level, and teachers were hired to teach the short sessions that were held in these schools. Because most of the parents were most interested in having the schools pass on the beliefs of the Puritan church, much of the teaching was centered on forcing students to memorize sections of the New England Primer and the Bible. Discipline was very strict, and teachers were allowed to beat their students. A child disciplined in school also needed to worry about a second beating when he or she arrived at home. Often the teacher or schoolmaster was thought of as an "assistant minister" in the community. Other young children who did not attend school might be taught by a mother in the home. At these so-called Dame Schools, there were also no specific qualifications for the women teaching their own and their neighbors' children. Beyond the early grades, a limited number of the more well-off boys attended a Latin grammar school where they might be taught by a master with more advanced education, but the emphasis remained on rote learning, primarily of Latin and Greek. Other young men became apprentices of local tradesmen. The master tradesmen had the responsibility not only of teaching the young men the skills of their trade but also of making certain that the apprentice was literate enough to carry on a business and to participate as a citizen.[3]

Unlike in New England where the Puritan denomination controlled most of the local governments, in the Middle Colonies, which included New York, Pennsylvania, New Jersey, and Delaware, there were a variety of denominations and people of differing national origins. While English was by far the primary language in New England, "it was said that thirteen languages were spoken in Dutch New Amsterdam before it became New York in 1664." In all of the Middle Colonies, it was individual churches that established most of the schools. Although there were a variety of denominations in each of the colonies, the Roman Catholic Church was dominant in Maryland while the Quakers were very strong in Pennsylvania. There was almost no colonial regulation of schools except that in several of the colonies, there was a licensing process for teachers. As in New England, Latin grammar schools were also created in the Middle Colonies. Teachers in these schools were usually ministers who had no specific congregation and whose main function was to prepare boys to go on to college with the idea that the students would someday become the church or governmental leaders of the colony.[4]

In the South before 1800, there were few formal schools. Children of the rich planter class hired private tutors, while other white children had limited opportunities for formal education. Needless to say, it was illegal in most southern colonies to educate the slaves. Although it is difficult to generalize about teachers in America during the more than two hundred years prior to Horace Mann's establishment of the first state-sponsored normal schools to train teachers, it is fair to say:

> Elementary school teachers in colonial America were very poorly prepared; more often than not, they had received no special training at all. The single qualification of most of them was that they themselves had been students. Most colonial college teachers, private tutors, Latin grammar school teachers, and academy teachers had received some kind of college education, usually at one of the well-established colleges or universities in Europe. A few had received their education at a colonial American college. . . . It was commonly believed that to be a teacher required only that the instructor know something about the subject matter to be taught; consequently, no teacher, regardless of the level taught, received training in the methodology of teaching.[5]

Colonial teachers were poorly paid, and many viewed their jobs as only temporary. Teaching was not a prestigious occupation, and young women who taught elementary school often did it only until they found a husband. Men frequently left teaching for careers in business or the ministry. Those who became "career teachers" were not often respected members of their community, and some lost their jobs for what was considered improper behavior. As in later years, it was not unusual for teachers to moonlight at other jobs such as digging graves, acting as a court messenger to serve summonses, or leading the church choir. Others accepted teaching positions as indentured servants who were expected to serve as instructors until they had paid off the cost of their passage to the new world.[6]

Even after the American Revolution, the preparation of teachers and the respect that they were given did not improve rapidly. As the state official responsible for education in Massachusetts, Horace Mann quickly observed the need for better training for teachers, and it became one of his major priorities. Of the teacher training institutions or normal schools that he would establish, Mann wrote:

> I believe Normal Schools to be a new instrumentality in the advancement of the race. I believe that, without them, Free Schools themselves would be shorn of their strength and their healing power, and would at length become mere charity schools, and thus die out in fact and in form.[7]

Not only was Mann interested in upgrading the preparation of teachers, but he also sought to elevate teachers to a more respected role in society. In pointing out the importance of improving the status of teachers, he noted that

> in our own country, where many paths, all brilliant with trophies of opulence and renown, allure the youth of the land, there is no other way to secure a fair proportion of the genius and erudition of the community for the department of teaching, than to requite its services with a fair share of all the honors and emoluments which society has to confer.[8]

The effort to raise the social standing of and remuneration for teachers gained support slowly in the latter half of the nineteenth century. Requirements for teacher training were raised as state-sponsored normal schools designed to train teachers were created in the half century after Mann's death. In addition, the number of private institutions that also trained teachers increased. Still, the twentieth-century historian Lawrence Cremin described the offerings of the early teacher-training institutions at the beginning of the twentieth century as being "meager at best." In some, the training would last only a single year. About teaching, Joseph Mayer Rice would write in 1893 that the "office of teachers in the American school . . . is perhaps the only one in the world that can be retained indefinitely in spite of the grossest negligence and incompetency." Unfortunately, some Americans would still suggest that because of tenure laws, not much has changed. Despite these criticisms of teachers, which have been with us since the beginning of our nation's history, progress has been made. The state normal school in Albany, New York, became the first of many such schools to create a four-year program for teachers. Private liberal arts colleges also established departments of education where courses in pedagogy were offered. In 1892, Teachers College at Columbia University in New York City was officially chartered in New York state and would become one of the nation's most respected teacher-training institutions. By 1900, a quarter of the colleges in the United States were "offering formal professional work in education."[9] Early in the twentieth century, a trend developed that saw hundreds of normal schools around the country being converted into four-year colleges. These converted colleges differed from the normal schools in the following ways:

- They offered a four-year curriculum (ultimately) versus one that was two or three years long.
- The curriculum included a general education program more comparable to the liberal education provided for any baccalaureate degree.
- There were increased requirements in a major field.

- A full program of professional studies in the history of education, curriculum and lesson design, and teaching methods was included.
- Several practica, culminating in student teaching, became required as part of the program. (In most colleges this included a full-time student teaching experience for a semester.)[10]

Undoubtedly Horace Mann would have been pleased with these developments. He also would have applauded the movement in the twentieth century that required that all teachers earn a bachelor's degree and, more recently in some states, a master's degree. Given his desire to raise the level of the academic requirements for teachers, I believe that he would have given strong support to the teacher certification laws that have been passed in every state. Because he introduced required examinations to complete the program in his normal schools, he would most likely have supported teacher certification tests in both the content areas and in pedagogy. Still, there are several other developments in teaching that might have caused him concern.

One such issue would be the development of national teacher unions. During his years as an educational bureaucrat in Massachusetts, Mann often found himself at odds with groups of teachers. For example, "in 1844, a group of 31 Boston schoolmasters publicly challenged Mann, contending that the abolition of corporal punishment would lead to anarchy in schools. The debate between the masters and the secretary continued for several months in the press and at the podium, with Mann the apparent but not uncontested victor."[11] That he would have wished to see these teachers organize and become powerful lobbying agents at the state and federal level is questionable. For him, perhaps the best teachers, at least at the elementary level, were women who were totally dedicated to children and to their job. It is doubtful that he could have imagined these paragons of humility and virtue carrying picket signs or participating in a strike.

Today more than 80 percent of the teachers in American belong to an affiliate of either the National Education Association or the

American Federation of Teachers.[12] With the formation of the National Education Association in 1857, educators, including school administrators, formed a national organization that is today one of the most powerful labor groups in America. In the preamble of its constitution, the National Education Association states that its purpose is to "elevate the character and advance the interest of the profession of teaching, and to promote the cause of popular education in the United States." Late in his life, Horace Mann supported the aims of the organization and "the group's desire to make teaching a profession, as opposed to a vocation." He was happy to also support the effort to replace lay leadership of schools with leadership provided by the members of the profession.[13] For much of its history, the organization included both teachers and school administrators. Although the official name of the group has changed several times, it continued to grow in influence in the late nineteenth and early twentieth centuries. In 1916, several groups of urban teachers, frustrated by their treatment by the boards of education in their cities, came together to form the American Federation of Teachers. This group was clearly a labor union, which would eventually become an affiliate of what is known as the American Federation of Labor and the Congress of Industrial Organizations. The American Federation of Teachers was only open to teachers, because the group felt that school administrators were representatives of the management.

The American Federation of Teachers adopted the union point of view regarding class struggle and accepted the need for militant tactics, including strikes. For many years, the National Education Association resisted the acceptance of such tactics since it continued to think of itself as a professional organization. With its assertive position with regard to improving the working conditions of teachers, the American Federation of Teachers grew rapidly, and in the decade beginning in 1910, its membership actually exceeded that of the National Education Association. Antiunion sentiment after World War I reversed this trend, and the National Education Association regained its position as the largest teacher group in America. Still, there is no question that the continued militancy of the American Federation of Teachers has pushed the larger organization to accept a similar position and tactics. Today, the two groups are quite similar in their objectives and also their methods for reaching these ends. A recent merger proposal was accepted by the American Federation of Teachers but was voted down by the delegates at the National Education Association's national convention. Some observers have suggested that the American Federation of Teachers' continued ties with the "blue collar" American Federation of Labor are not appreciated by many of the more conservative members of the National Education Association.[14]

Politically, both organizations have aligned themselves with the Democratic Party. Since the passage of New Deal legislation in the 1930s protecting the right of workers to engage in collective bargaining, teacher organizations have been a major force within the Democratic Party. This support has been strengthened by the willingness of Democratic politicians to continue to increase the amount of money being spent on public education. Other teacher-friendly laws such as tenure legislation at the state level have only strengthened the relationship.

Horace Mann was not a Democrat and he worried about conflict in our society between workers and management. He sincerely hoped that the common schools would have a positive effect on reducing class conflict by giving all children the opportunity to attend school together. For him, the common schools would be a place where the children of the working class would have the same opportunity to succeed as those whose parents were well-off professionals or business owners. He might well have seen labor unions as a divisive factor in our society.

While he would have been concerned about teachers forming militant labor unions, he would undoubtedly have supported many of the objectives of these groups. He certainly favored better pay and fringe benefits, which would attract more able individuals to the profession. Increased compensation would also help to encourage teachers to stay in the profession. In Horace Mann's lifetime, teacher turnover was a problem just as it is today.

Mann also would have agreed with the unions' support for increasing the qualifications for entering teachers. In addition, he would be happy with union efforts to provide their members with additional professional development opportunities after entering the field.

On the other hand, he might have had reservations about the current teacher tenure laws, which are considered by many to go too far in providing job security for teachers who are incompetent. He probably also would have questioned the seniority clauses in some teacher contracts that limit school managers in the placement of teachers within the district and in deciding which teachers should be laid off when that becomes necessary. It is difficult to predict what his thoughts would have been about the huge amounts of money that the current unions are spending on lobbying efforts at both the state and federal levels. As a state employee and as a congressman, he might have resented the power that organizations gain from their liberal campaign contributions.

Despite his unquestionable commitment to public education, one could legitimately question whether our current teacher unions would have been comfortable supporting Horace Mann either when he was serving as the secretary of the Board of Education in Massachusetts or when he was a congressman. There is one issue upon which there would be no conflict between teacher unions and Horace Mann. The records of both show strong support for improving teacher salaries and fringe benefits.

That teachers are better off today than they were during the lifetime of Horace Mann is indisputable. Whether Mann would accept the current levels of remuneration for teachers as being fair and appropriate is another question. Although teacher salaries rose at an uneven pace during the first eight decades of the twentieth century, progress in the last quarter century has not been encouraging for the profession. Pam Grossman, in a study of the trends in teacher salaries in recent years, concluded that "by and large teacher salaries have not kept up with inflation." In fact, in 1990–91 and 2000–01, salaries actually declined.[15] Another study of salaries during the past ten years found that "the mean of classroom teachers' average salaries in unadjusted dollars rose from $36,531 in 1993–94 to $45,646 in 2003–04. After factoring in cost-of-living increases, however, the average teacher salary actually fell by $871 or 1.87 percent during the past ten years." At the same time, it was reported that "the average inflation-adjusted salary of superintendents, for example, jumped more than twelve percent during the same period. Principals' salaries have risen by more than four percent to $86,160. Even the pay of such support personnel as custodians and bus drivers rose nearly five percent."[16]

Still it is true that with teacher salaries, there are tremendous differences depending on the location of the school. Because of our heavy reliance on the property tax, most suburban districts are able to pay their teachers higher salaries while urban teachers lag behind. The lowest salary schedules tend to be in poor, remote, rural areas. The difference in teacher salaries between states is also dramatic. During the 2002–03 school year, the states with the highest average pay were California, $55,693; Michigan, $54,020; Connecticut, $53,962; New Jersey $53,872; and the District of Columbia, $53,194. The states with lowest average pay were South Dakota, $32,414; Montana, $35,754; Mississippi, $35,135; North Dakota, $33,869; and Oklahoma, $33,277. Beginning salaries ranged from $37,401 in Alaska to $23,052 in Montana.[17] Perhaps even a more significant problem is captured in a headline for a story in *Education Week* that reads, "Salary Totals Found Lower in Poorer Schools." Even though most educators would agree that high-poverty schools should receive the most resources, nationwide we continue to spend more money on children in the affluent suburbs.[18]

Comparisons with other occupations also put teacher salaries in a less-than-positive light. The American Federation of Teachers in a study in 2000–01 placed the average teacher salary in the nation at $43,250. At the same time, average wages for selected white-collar occupations were listed as $52,664 for a mid-level accountant; $71,155 for a computer system analyst; and $74,920 for an engineer.[19]

Although certainly not the only factor, low wages have most likely contributed to the fact that "nearly one of six public school teachers nationwide didn't come back to their school systems last year." While salaries are important, working conditions might be an even more significant problem in causing a high attrition rate in the teaching profession. Many people would agree with the sentiments expressed in an article published by the Durham Public Education Network, which stated:

> Teachers often don't feel that they are respected in their profession or that they get the assistance and training they need. . . . A poor work environment can result from such problems as teachers having to buy their own supplies to principals putting students who speak limited English in their classes without properly training teachers how to educate them. Often, new teachers are left to navigate their new profession by themselves with little help from those more experienced. That can lead to feelings of loneliness and frustration, and eventual abandonment of the profession.[20]

There is no question that high turnover rate and low salaries remain a problem for teachers. Still, there is a development that is currently raising the professional status of teachers in every state. Historically, teacher certification has been a prerogative of state governments, but because of the creation of the National Board of Teaching Standards, there now is an opportunity for experienced teachers to receive what is being accepted in many places as national certification. The National Board of Teaching Standards is committed to "advance[ing] the quality of teaching and learning" by:

- maintaining high and rigorous standards for what accomplished teachers should know and be able to do,
- providing a national voluntary system certifying teachers who meet these standards, and
- advocating related education reforms to integrate National Board Certification into American education and to capitalize on the expertise of National Board Certified Teachers.[21]

Experienced teachers may now choose to enter a very rigorous process and achieve this new certification. Once this is completed, National Board Certified Teachers are usually given additional recognition within their district, and many boards of education have chosen to encourage the process by paying the cost and even adding an additional stipend to the teacher's salary.

At the same time that we are having this movement toward national certification, there seems to have been a period of relatively peaceful relations between teacher unions and their school districts. The last several decades have seen a reduction in strikes and often an increase in cooperation within school districts. In many ways, the teaching profession is at a crossroads. Poor economic times, which could be accompanied by stagnant or lower salaries, could result in more militant union tactics. On the other hand, teachers might make as their primary goal the effort to raise the level of respect of their profession.

In any case, although Horace Mann and the other founders of the public school movement would be impressed with the academic background and pedagogical skills of today's teachers, they would not be satisfied with the current state of the profession. The high attrition rate and the comparatively low wages for teachers would be seen as problems that need to be addressed. These issues are just two of the concerns expressed in a document that many believe launched the educational reform movement in which we are currently involved. For many, the *A Nation at Risk* report was a significant turning point in the history of education in the United States. For that reason, it is important to look at the trends that have emerged since the publication of this report to try to determine if these initiatives are consistent with the initial vision for public schools in America.

NOTES

1. Jack L. Nelson, Stuart B. Palonsky, and Mary Rose McCarthy, *Critical Issues in Education: Dialogues and Dialectics* (Boston: McGraw-Hill, 2004), 159.

2. James A. Johnson, Victor L. Dupuis, Diann Musial, Gene E. Hall, and Donna M. Gollnick, *Introduction to the Foundations of American Education* (Boston: Allyn and Bacon, 1996), 323.

3. David Schuman, *American Schools, American Teachers* (Boston: Pearson Education, Inc., 2004), 25–28.

4. John D. Pulliam and James J. Van Patten, *History of Education in America* (Upper Saddle River, NJ: Prentice-Hall, Inc., 1999), 58–61.

5. Johnson, et al., *Introduction,* 323–24.

6. Johnson, et al., *Introduction*, 324.

7. Joy Elmer Morgan, *Horace Mann, His Ideas and Ideals* (Washington, DC: The National Home Library Foundation, 1936), 135.

8. Morgan, *Horace Mann,* 138.

9. Lawrence A. Cremin, *The Transformation of the School* (New York: Vintage Books, 1964), 169–70.

10. Charles R. Coble, "Who's in Charge Here: The Changing Landscape of Teacher Preparation in America," Education Commission of the States, September 2004, www.ecs.org/clearinghouse/54/36/5436.htm, 5 (accessed 14 March 2005).

11. Gerald L. Gutek, *Historical and Philosophical Foundations of Education* (Upper Saddle River, NJ: Pearson Education, Inc., 2005), 230.

12. Nelson, Palonsky, and McCarthy, *Critical Issues in Education*, 427.

13. Peters S. Hlebowitsh, *Foundations of American Education* (Belmont, CA: Wadsworth Group, 2001), 232.

14. Hlebowitsh, *Foundations*, 238–40.

15. David T. Gordon, ed., *A Nation Reformed?* (Cambridge, MA: Harvard Education Press, 2003), 76.

16. Catherine Gewertz, "Pay it Backward," *Teacher Magazine*, September 2004, www.teachermagazine.org/tmstory.cfm?slug=01Salaries.h16 (accessed 17 September 2004), 1.

17. "Teacher Salaries Remain Stagnant but Health Insurance Costs Soar," *AFT Press Center*, 15 July 2004, www.aft.org/presscenter/relaeases/2004/071504.htm (accessed 7 February 2005), 1.

18. Jeff Archer, "Salary Totals Found Lower in Poor Schools," *EdWeek*, 16 February 2005, www.edweek.org/ew/articles/2005/02/16/23salaries.h24.html (accessed 16 February 2005), 1.

19. Michael Podgursky, "Fringe Benefits," *Education Next*, www.educationnext.org/20033/71.html (accessed 7 February 2005), 1.

20. Nikole Hanna-Jones "Group targets teacher exodus," *New Observer*, 30 December 2004, www.newobserver.com/news/story/1972256p-8346406c.html (accessed 1 February 2005), 1–2.

21. "About NBPTS," National Board for Professional Teaching Standards, www.nbpts.org/about/index.cfm (accessed 7 February 2005), 1.

13

THE DIRECTION

The educational trends that are guiding school reform at the beginning of the twenty-first century began in the 1980s. At that time, there was a feeling among many Americans that all was not well in our nation. In a chapter on the Reagan Revolution, historian Harold Evans described the situation this way:

> At the end of the seventies, America simmered with accumulated fears and frustrations. The country seemed ripe for political revolution. Middle-class families were already worried about rising unemployment and street crime, permissiveness and race relations.[1]

The economy was faltering, and we were seemingly faring poorly in our economic competition with Japan and the countries of Western Europe. Our automobile and steel companies were experiencing a dramatic decline in their market share. In 1981, our annual inflation rate stood at 12.5 percent. To stem rising prices, the Federal Reserve had raised the prime interest rate to 21.5 percent. At the same time, to the consternation of government economists, prices continued to rise and the unemployment rate in the nation jumped to 10.7 percent.[2]

As businessmen and government officials sought the reasons for our economic problems, one of the aspects of our society that was pinpointed was the public schools. This reaction could be compared to the way many reacted to the Soviet Union's surprise launching of

Sputnik in 1957. As a result of the Soviet Union's triumph in space, Congress reacted quickly to bolster science education in our schools.

Public schools would not have been such a convenient target if there had not already been many underlying doubts about their effectiveness. During the 1960s, schools engaged in a number of experimental innovations. So-called open schools, or schools without walls to separate classrooms, had been built to allow more flexibility in programming. High schools had introduced numerous electives to appeal to student interests, and many believed that these new offerings had diluted the high school curriculum. There was a feeling among some critics that the so-called "basics"—English, history, science, and math—were being deemphasized. Some high schools had introduced an open campus and even created smoking lounges for students. Studies showed that parents were concerned about discipline in their schools, and others worried when they read the results of test score comparisons with other countries.

In response to the concerns of both the business community and the general public about problems in our schools, a whole series of national reports articulated the problems and offered a variety of solutions. Of these reports, most historians point to the *A Nation at Risk* report released in 1983 as being the primary influence in instigating reform in education during the past twenty years. Respected education historian Diane Ravitch has written:

> *A Nation at Risk* was a landmark of education reform literature. Countless previous reports by prestigious national commissions had been ignored by the national press and the general public. *A Nation at Risk* was different. Written in stirring language that the general public could understand, the report warned that schools had not kept pace with the changes in society and the economy and that the nation would suffer if education were not dramatically improved for all children. It also asserted that lax academic standards were correlated with lax behavior standards and that neither should be ignored.[3]

The report was written because of the initiative and leadership of Ronald Reagan's secretary of education, Terrel Bell. Despite the fact that President Reagan and the Republican Party were committed to dismantling the Department of Education, which had only been established a few years earlier by Jimmy Carter, Bell went ahead and appointed a distinguished panel to study the condition of the nation's schools and to make appropriate recommendations for reform. After months of data collection and hearings, the report was introduced to the public by the president. The introductory section of the document would be reported nationwide. Newspapers, television, and periodicals all quoted the warning in the introduction of the report, which said:

> Our nation is at risk. Our once unchallenged prominence in commerce, industry, science, and technological innovation is being overtaken by competitors throughout the world. . . . If an unfriendly foreign power had attempted to impose on America the mediocre educational performance that exists today, we might well have viewed it as an act of war. As it stands, we have allowed this to happen to ourselves. We have even squandered the gains in student achievement made in the wake of the Sputnik challenge. Moreover, we have dismantled essential support systems, which helped make those gains possible. We have, in effect, been committing an act of unthinking, unilateral educational disarmament.[4]

Leaders, especially at the state level, took these words seriously. In part, this occurred because of the focus on education during the 1984 presidential campaign. As part of his reelection campaign, President Reagan embraced the report in numerous campaign speeches. The attention given the report motivated state governments to appoint their own commissions to study the status of the schools in their states. Members of the business community also showed a willingness to participate in these reform efforts. The *A Nation at Risk* report outlined a number of serious problems in a section that was titled "Indicators of Risk":

- International comparisons of student achievement, completed a decade ago, reveal that on nineteen academic tests American students were never first or second and, in comparison with other industrialized nations, were last seven times.

- Some twenty-three million American adults are functionally illiterate by the simplest tests of everyday reading, writing, and comprehension.
- About 13 percent of all seventeen-year-olds in the United States can be considered functionally illiterate.
- Average achievement of high school students on most standardized tests is now lower than twenty-six years ago when Sputnik was launched.
- The College Board's Scholastic Aptitude Test (SAT) demonstrates virtually unbroken decline from 1963 to 1980. Average verbal scores fell over fifty points and average mathematics scores dropped nearly forty points.
- There has been a steady decline in science achievement scores of U.S. seventeen-year-olds as measured by national assessments of science in 1969, 1973, and 1977.
- The average tested achievement of students graduating from college is also lower.[5]

The report was especially critical of science education. It quoted educational researcher Paul Hurd, who concluded after doing a national study on student achievement in science that "we are raising a new generation of Americans that is scientifically and technologically illiterate." John Slaughter, a former director of the National Science Foundation, was also quoted as saying that the nation has "a growing chasm between a small scientific and technological elite and a citizenry ill-informed, indeed uninformed, on issues with a science component."[6]

In another section, the following issues were highlighted:

- a decrease in time students spend on homework
- the lack of time actually spent by schools on math and science instruction
- the lack of instruction, especially at the elementary level, in foreign languages
- the increased number of nonacademic electives allowed for high school credit

- the use of "minimum competency examinations," which is leading to low academic expectations for students
- a reduction in academic requirements for admission to college
- boring and poorly written textbooks[7]

Because of these and other findings, the commission that wrote the report would make a series of recommendations. Many of these proposals would become the basis for most of the educational reform initiatives during the last two decades. A close examination of what has been happening might be summarized as follows:

1. We have seen a movement that has been labeled "back to basics."
2. In implementing this trend, the idea of creating curriculum standards has occurred in every state. These curriculum standards articulate what students should be expected to know and be able to do in each curriculum area.
3. To ensure that these standards are being taught in our classrooms, there has been a movement to introduce "high-stakes" tests to assess student learning.
4. To make certain that schools take these initiatives seriously, systems have been put in place requiring that test results and comparisons of test results between districts be made public.

All of the above initiatives were suggested in the *A Nation at Risk* report. A fifth trend has emerged that was not included in the commission's recommendations but has gained significant support. As noted earlier, school choice in many forms has been introduced into our system in recent years. Since that initiative and Horace Mann's possible reaction to it were discussed in an earlier chapter, the other trends that are part of the current reform movement will be considered here.

The *A Nation at Risk* report was clear in its specific recommendation that high school curriculums include:

- four years of English
- three years of mathematics

- three years of science
- three years of social studies
- six months of computer science
- two years of foreign language (strongly recommended in addition to those taken earlier)[8]

This curriculum, which is labeled New Basics, provided a blueprint for many states that were at the time requiring only one year of math and science, no foreign language, and little in the way of computer instruction. It should be noted that although the report mentions foreign language instruction, it is not considered one of the New Basics. The commission went on to attempt to articulate what might today be called curriculum standards. For example, it said that a science curriculum should teach the following:

- The concepts, laws, and processes of the physical and biological sciences
- The methods of scientific inquiry and reasoning
- The application of scientific and technological development
- The social and environmental implications of scientific and technological development[9]

School districts' attempt to emphasize the basics outlined by the report is clear, as most states have increased the number of science and math courses required for graduation and have also included in their required curriculums some form of computer instruction. At the same time, it was recommended that specific goals or standards for all basic subjects be developed in every state. The trend emphasizing language arts (reading, writing, speaking, and listening) at the elementary and middle school levels has been dramatically accelerated because of the mandatory testing in these areas required by the No Child Left Behind legislation. How Horace Mann would react to the current "back to basics" movement raises a question about which it is difficult to speculate.

Knowing for sure how he would react to issues related to high school curriculum is especially difficult because most of his writing related to what we would call grades 1–8, while the *A Nation at Risk* report concentrated heavily on high school curriculum. It is clear from Mann's writing and speeches that he wished schools to do much more than teach basic skills. He talked often about the schools' need to ingrain in students such qualities as "industry," "integrity," "spiritual elevation," and a sense of duty to all humanity. While he also spoke about strengthening children's minds in the "exact sciences," he also believed that schools must "save" children "from the vicious association of depraved habits." Schools, for Mann, should cause students to be "less selfish" and to develop "a more ardent love of man and a reverence for God."[10] For him, these goals would be part of what we call today "character" or "values" education. These were essential aspects for him of any public school curriculum.

One difference in what Horace Mann envisioned in the area of character education is that to him it should be tied to what he saw as agreed-upon Christian teachings. It is likely that for him, the current emphasis on the role of the schools in teaching basic skills would be too narrow. He believed that the "ultimate object and end of public education was to form character."[11]

In addition, Mann would have pointed to the need for schools to provide what we call today citizenship education. The first sentence in his ninth annual report to the Massachusetts Board of Education said that "one of the highest and most valuable objects, to which the influences of a school can be made conducive, consists in training our children to self-government."[12] Certainly for Horace Mann, citizenship education would be one of the basics.

After the initiative of returning to basics, the second important trend that has occurred during the past two decades is what has been labeled the "standards movement." For many, it was not enough for schools to merely spend more time on basic subjects. It was felt, especially by those in the business community, that we must clearly articulate what students should know and be able to do in each of the curriculum areas. Without clearly specifying the goals, we can never know whether our students are learning what society thinks is important. A major debate occurred in this country over whether these curriculum standards in each subject should be developed at the national level. Those supporting national standards pointed out that the only way we could compare students from different states would be if the nation had agreed-upon national education outcomes. These individuals argued that without national standards, the great variation in the effectiveness of state education programs would continue. On the other side of this issue were conservatives who saw national curriculum standards as an encroachment by the federal government into what constitutionally and historically had been a function of the state and local governments. In the end, this viewpoint prevailed, and we now have fifty sets of curriculum standards. Every state has identified the curriculum objectives it is seeking to accomplish in each of the basic subjects.

Although Horace Mann would not have quarreled with the idea of identifying what children should learn, he undoubtedly would have added several categories of standards. While one could probably find references to character education and citizenship education somewhere in the various state plans, Mann would have made these areas the centerpieces of what schools should be doing. Citizenship education would not be just one of many goals listed under the social studies standards.

The term "standards" is also used in education discussions to define the level of accomplishment we expect of students. Critics, including the authors of the *A Nation at Risk* report, have written about the need to measure student learning. This goal has led to the third of the four trends that have dominated recent reform in public education. Schools have been prodded into accepting new testing programs, labeled "high-stakes testing," which seek to determine whether they are truly teaching their state's curriculum standards. To be effective, these tests have to be made to matter to students, faculty, school administrators, parents, and taxpayers. In order that the tests be taken seriously by students, state governments and individual districts have tied test results to such meaningful educational decisions as grade level retention, eligibility for extracurricular activities, and even high school graduation. For teachers, the results of student testing can affect their job evaluations and, ultimately, a tenure appointment. In some states, teachers are being rewarded with extra pay if their students demonstrate outstanding results in state tests.

The fourth trend is tied directly to high-stakes testing. Schools are increasingly being held accountable for their students' scores on tests. These test results are widely publicized and also include comparisons between districts. Administrators and members of boards of education are also feeling significant community pressure if their schools' test scores are not improving. With the passage of the No Child Left Behind Act, districts are facing penalties for failure to show improvement for all of their students. Accountability has placed a spotlight on the performance of each and every school. It is even possible that schools that do not improve will eventually be closed. Standards, high-stakes testing, and school accountability are initiatives designed to foster school improvement, at least as it is measured by the results of academic tests.

Horace Mann, like every other educator, was committed to improving schools and increasing student learning. He was not against a well-defined academic curriculum or testing, and he would not have been a party to protecting poorly functioning schools. What he might well have objected to is an overemphasis on testing in selected academic areas. For Mann, the primary goals of schools could not be measured in a typical paper-and-pencil test. It is undeniably true that neither he nor subsequent generations of educators have been able to create appropriate measurement tools for the efforts of schools to promote character and citizenship education. Even without such measurements, Horace Mann would maintain that these goals are truly the primary functions of public education. Success in achieving high test scores in the basic academic subjects would never have been enough for Horace Mann. If public schools are to indeed be "the greatest discovery made by man," they must do much more. For him, schools could make "nine-tenths of the crimes in the penal code . . . obsolete; the long catalog of human ills will be abridged; men will walk more safely by day; every pillow will be more inviolable by night; property, life, and character will be held by a stronger tenure; all rational hopes respecting the future brightened."[13] Although few Americans in the twenty-first century would consider these aspirations as even approachable, many would agree that schools need to do more than return to basics, establish standards, develop high-stakes tests, and make schools accountable. This approach to education reform was instigated by the *A Nation at Risk* report, but it has more recently been given a major boost by the No Child Left Behind Law signed by President Bush in 2002.

NOTES

1. Harold Evans, *The American Century* (New York: Alfred A. Knopf, Inc., 1998), 612.

2. The Editors of Time-Life Books, *Pride and Prosperity: The 80's* (Richmond: Time-Life Books, 1999), 24–26.

3. Diane Ravitch, *Left Back: A Century of Battles Over School Reform* (New York: Touchstone, 2000), 411–12.

4. Myra Pollack Sadker and David Miller Sadker, *Teachers, Schools, and Society* (Boston: McGraw-Hill, 2000), 148–49.

5. U.S. Department of Education, The National Commission on Excellence in Education, *A Nation at Risk: The Imperative for Educational Reform*, April 1983, Introduction, 2–3.

6. *A Nation at Risk,* Introduction, 2.

7. *A Nation at Risk*, Findings, 1–2.

8. *A Nation at Risk*, Recommendations, 1.

9. *A Nation at Risk*, Recommendations, 2.

10. Joy Elmer Morgan, *Horace Mann, His Ideas and Ideals* (Washington, DC: National Home Library Foundation, 1936), 133–34.

11. Jonathan Messerli, *Horace Mann: A Biography* (New York: Alfred A. Knopf, 1972), 264.

12. Lawrence A. Cremin, ed., *The Republic and the School: Horace Mann on the Education of Free Men* (New York: Bureau of Publications, Teachers College, Columbia University, 1957), 57.

13. Morgan, *Horace Mann, His Ideas and Ideals*, 132–33.

14

THE LAW

No one, least of all Horace Mann, could argue with the purpose of the No Child Left Behind law. This very complex legislation, which runs over six hundred pages, was signed by President Bush on January 8, 2002. With bipartisan support, the law created a new role for the federal government in the field of public education. Technically, it is a reauthorization of the Elementary and Secondary Education Act, which was enacted as part of President Lyndon Johnson's War on Poverty in 1965. The No Child Left Behind Act uses the federal aid granted under Title I of the Elementary and Secondary Act to require states and individual school districts to comply with a whole new set of regulations. Failure to do so can cause a district to lose a significant amount of federal aid. Among the mandates included in the No Child Left Behind law are the following:

- *Annual Testing*
  By the 2005–06 school year, states must begin testing students in grades 3–8 annually in reading and mathematics. By 2007–08 they must test students in science at least once in elementary, middle, and high school.
- *Academic Progress*
  States must bring all students up to the "proficient" level on state tests by the 2013–14 school year. Individual schools must meet the state's "adequate yearly progress" targets toward this goal

(based on a formula spelled out in the law) both for their student populations as a whole and for certain demographic subgroups. If a school receiving Title I funding fails to meet the target two years in a row, it must be provided technical assistance and its students must be offered a choice of other public schools to attend.

- *Report Cards*
  Starting with the 2002–03 school year, states must furnish annual report cards showing a range of information, including student achievement data broken down by subgroup and information on the performance of school districts. Districts must provide similar report cards showing school-by-school data.
- *Teacher Qualifications*
  By the end of the 2005–06 school year, every teacher in core content areas working in a public school must be "highly qualified" in each subject he or she teaches. Under the law, "highly qualified" generally means that a teacher is certified and demonstrably proficient in his or her subject matter.[1]

Almost since the day of its passage, the law has been a source of controversy. Despite the fact that Democrats, including John Kerry and his fellow senator from Massachusetts, Edward Kennedy, voted for the bill, during the 2004 presidential campaign both were quick to criticize what they believed was President Bush's failure to seek from Congress adequate funds to ensure the success of the legislation. State officials as well as local educational leaders have also pointed to the added cost to school districts if they are to sincerely seek to implement all of the many facets of No Child Left Behind. Robert J. Sternberg has summarized many of the major criticisms of the legislation. Along with the lack of adequate financial support, he lists the following problems with the law:

- *It Penalizes Schools with Children from Diverse Backgrounds*
  Schools with children of lower socioeconomic status will be at a disadvantage in almost any rigid standard of accountability. The same will be true for schools with many children for whom English is a second language.

- *It Penalizes Schools with Children Having Diverse Learning Skills*
  Schools having many children with learning disabilities or other
  diverse learning needs will almost inevitably fare poorly in a
  rigid accountability system that expects to have a single yard-
  stick for all students. So these schools, too, will be penalized.
- *It Encourages Cheating*
  Because the stakes for high scores are so high, schools are inadvertently encouraged to fudge the data, give children answers to tests, or make various attempts to exclude children
  from testing who, according to the act, should be tested.
- *It Encourages Schools to Promote Dropping Out*
  Ironically, the "No Child" law inadvertently encourages schools
  to encourage their weaker students to drop out. In this way,
  those students' test scores will not reduce scores for the school.
  Student dropouts among low scorers actually have been in-
  creasing, arguably as a direct result of the legislation.
- *The Law Assumes that Knowledge of the Three Rs Is Supreme*
  Schooling is more and more emphasizing the traditional three
  Rs of reading, writing, and arithmetic. As a result of the legis-
  lation, less emphasis is being placed on the arts, social studies,
  and physical education.
- *The Law Assumes that Conventional Tests Are Some Kind of
  Panacea for the Nation's Education Woes*
  Relatively few countries in the world use the kinds of multiple-
  choice and short-answer tests that are so popular in the United
  States. They believe that such tests can measure only superfi-
  cial levels of knowledge.
- *The Law Is Causing Our Schools to Spend Significant Amounts of
  Time and Effort in Teaching to the Test*
  To a large extent, many of our classes have become test prepa-
  ration courses. Schools are teaching very specific skills related
  to test-taking that will be of relatively little use outside of the
  statewide testing program.
- *The Law Is Dividing Rather Than Unifying the World of Education*
  The No Child Left Behind legislation was originally passed with
  bipartisan support, but it has already lost the support of many

Democrats and some Republicans. Opposition is also strong among national organizations of teachers, administrators, and school boards.[2]

Nel Noddings was more blunt in her criticisms of the law when she wrote that "the No Child Left Behind Act is a bad law, and a bad law is not made better by fully funding it." She adds to the list of criticisms of the legislation the following:

- The cost of implementing the legislation is so high that throughout the country, states and districts are considering rejecting federal funds rather than trying to enforce the law.
- The law employs a view of motivation that many in education find objectionable. As educators, we should not use threats, punishments, and pernicious comparisons to "motivate our students," but that is how the No Child Left Behind law treats the school establishment.
- The high-stakes testing associated with the law seems to be demoralizing teachers, students, and administrators. A good law does not demoralize good people.[3]

As controversial as the provisions of the law are, the attempts so far to judge its effectiveness are also a source of additional conflict. As early as September 24, 2004, the then Secretary of Education, Rod Paige, was quoted as saying, "I am pleased to report that the law is making a positive difference in millions of lives . . . there is clear evidence of success, noticeable patterns of change, and upbeat reports all across the nation from a variety of sources. Simply stated: The law is working."[4] The secretary's contention was supported in an article published in *Education Week* in October 2004 that noted that "since the federal No Child Left Behind law was enacted nearly three years ago, almost half the states have seen rising math scores on their state exams." Daria Hall, a policy analyst for the *Education Trust*, a Washington-based research and advocacy group, reported that reading scores had also improved among fourth and fifth graders in fifteen of twenty-three states. These results were disputed in another study mentioned in the article, which "paints a contrasting picture of declining or flattening reading achievement in some states."[5] Professor Bruce Fuller, the lead author of the second study, was almost immediately criticized for his findings, which Secretary Paige suggested might have been "politically motivated."[6]

A more recent survey, released in February 2005, was also less than complimentary concerning the impact of the law to date. After holding hearings in six cities, a bipartisan panel of lawmakers from a number of states concluded that the No Child Left Behind legislation was "a flawed, convoluted, and unconstitutional education reform initiative that had usurped state and local control of public schools." The panel, sponsored by the National Conference of State Legislators, stated in their final report that "under N.C.L.B., the federal government's role has become excessively intrusive in the day-to-day operations of public education."[7]

Still another report, done by the Rand Corporation, concluded that students in the upper elementary grades have little hope of reaching the language arts achievement goals set for 2014. The study stated that "inadequate progress is being made to meet these requirements." A spokesman for the United States Education Department responded to the study by saying, "we're only a few years into these reforms, and just because we're not there yet doesn't mean we abandon kids and the goal of having them all at grade level—it means we work harder."[8]

Perhaps one of the most disturbing concerns regarding the impact of the law is voiced by critic Alfie Kohn. He suggests that the law's emphasis on curriculum standards and high-stakes testing is creating in our school children an emotional state that alternates "between anxiety and boredom." He argues that our students have been placed on the "receiving end of a curriculum specified by powerful and distant others. Those in poor neighborhoods can count on sitting through prefabricated lessons, often minutely scripted, whose purpose is not to promote thinking, much less the joy of discovery, but to raise test scores." He ends the article with the question, "Why are our schools not places of joy? Because too many of us respond to outrageous edicts by saying 'fine.'"[9]

With all of its critics, one might question whether this law will be changed or repealed. At this time such a result seems unlikely. Even prior to his victory in the 2004 election, President Bush announced his desire to expand the law by adding new required high school examinations. The focus of these new tests would be in the fields of math and science.[10] Following the election, in his 2005 State of the Union address, the president restated his support for the extension of testing into the high schools. Reaction to this plan has come from a number of sources. Many Democrats who have been hearing the concerns of teacher unions, state legislators, and school boards seem unready to extend the testing program at this time. They are joined in opposition to the president's proposal by a group of conservative Republicans who feel that the law has already gone too far in pushing the federal government into areas that should be controlled by state and local government.[11]

The law had additional bad press when in January of 2005, it was reported that the Department of Education was paying conservative commentator Armstrong Williams $240,000 to "tout" the No Child Left Behind Act. When this became public knowledge, President Bush said that he knew nothing about the plan and admitted that it was inappropriate.[12]

Even though controversy continues to plague the implementation of the law, it is possible that the Education Department will in the future become more willing to consider modifications. Secretary Paige has resigned his position and has been replaced by Margaret Spellings, who "has shown a willingness to work with state and local officials on what they consider to be some of the toughest requirements of . . . No Child Left Behind." She has said that it is her intention "to balance states' rights to control schools with the federal government's responsibility to reduce the achievement gap between suburban white and urban minority students."[13]

Whatever approach the new secretary takes, it appears that the system created under the law is being put in place and is functioning. In the words of Lynn Olson, writing in *Education Week*, "Despite ongoing complaints, the federal No Child Left Behind Act has become implanted in the culture of America's public school system."

By the end of 2004, twenty-three states had already begun testing reading and math in grades 3–8. This is well ahead of the mandated deadline, which is to begin testing during the 2005–2006 school year. An equal number of states have begun science testing, which is not required until 2007.[14]

While states are moving forward in their efforts to comply with the law, the effort to amend the legislation or at least change the current enforcement policies continues. In late 2004, "a coalition of 30 national organizations called on Congress to make major changes in the law, including how academic progress is measured, substitution of sanctions that do not have a consistent record of success, and a funding increase."[15] From all indications, President Bush and a Republican-dominated Congress are not going to be easily persuaded to make significant changes in the bill in the near future.

There are a number of facets of the No Child Left Behind Act that I believe would have been supported by Horace Mann and the other early supporters of the public school movement. Certainly they would have seen the effort to improve the preparation of teachers as an important initiative. The fact that Mann and others spent a good deal of time and effort in seeking additional money for schools would lead one to assume that they would have favored additional funding for education, especially funds earmarked for at-risk students. The effort to develop curriculum standards at the state level is also consistent with Mann's efforts to create a common curriculum in his home state of Massachusetts.

As a congressman and later a well-traveled educational authority, Horace Mann might well have concluded that national standards were preferable to state standards. His desire while in Congress to establish a federal education agency would suggest that he was prepared for some sort of role for the federal government in public education. By even considering such a possibility, he was far ahead of his contemporaries in the mid-nineteenth century.

There are several other areas where one can only guess at Mann's reaction to the law. Even though he was not averse to testing students or teachers, it must be remembered that for him, the primary objectives for the public school would be difficult to assess. A student's personal values or his or her commitment to the democratic system are outcomes that cannot easily be determined using a test. He most likely would have agreed with Richard Rothstein, who wrote in the *American School Board Journal* that "standardized tests are fine for some purposes, but they can't assess creativity, insight, or many other important traits."[16] Finally he would also worry about a trend that Rothstein suggested was forcing "teachers to concentrate on what is tested and ignore the equally important curricular areas that don't lend themselves to cheap assessment."[17]

Probably Horace Mann would also be concerned if it is indeed true that high-stakes testing is creating anxiety and boredom in our classrooms. He would certainly wish to challenge students academically but would not want to do so by creating fear. He fought to end corporal punishment in Massachusetts because he thought it was a negative form of motivation. Although he might not feel as strongly about motivating students through fear of academic failure, he might become concerned if this is the primary way we are attempting to ensure student learning.

Horace Mann might also worry about the mandates for testing in reading, math, and science if they caused a reduction in the instruction in other subjects. He would have been especially upset reading a headline such as the one that stated, "Instructors say social studies suffering because of No Child Left Behind Act." In the article, a spokesman for the National Council for Social Studies is quoted as saying, "the worst thing that has ever happened to social studies has been the No Child Left Behind law." The article suggests that the problem is most pronounced for students in schools where children have difficulty succeeding on the required tests in reading and math.[18]

Because social studies is the likely place in the curriculum where students would be receiving instruction for citizenship, Mann would feel that any reduction in emphasis in this area would be detrimental to one of the primary functions of the public schools. He would undoubtedly question as well the fact that although the law does punish schools considered unsafe by allowing parents to transfer their children out of school, it does not create any type of mandated character education program. There is no question that for him, the school must do more than teach basic skills; it must also become for society the "wheel of progress." Horace Mann's extraordinary faith in schools caused him to believe "that the great body of vices and crimes which now saddens and torments the community, may be dislodged and driven out from amongst us, by such improvements in our present Common School system."[19]

Even though he was never as explicit as we might like in suggesting how these laudable objectives could be reached, it is very likely that teaching and testing students in the basic skills would not be sufficient for Horace Mann. In considering what is occurring in some schools, I believe that he would have supported the current experimental programs in character and citizenship education, such as "service learning." These programs allow students to serve as volunteers in various places in the community. He would also applaud the efforts of some schools that require students to observe and participate in local government projects.

If social studies teachers are worried about the impact of No Child Left Behind, the same also might be said of instructors in the fields of music, art, physical education, and health. Should these curriculum areas begin to become shortchanged in our schools, it would undoubtedly concern Horace Mann and the other early supporters of the common school.

Like many educators today, Horace Mann would most likely have some doubts about the possible results of the No Child Left Behind legislation. He would support the goals of the law and certainly the additional money promised to help less fortunate children. At the same time, he would have empathy for and probably support the critics who attack the design of the programs that have been established to meet the objectives.

Since the first public schools were established, people have debated, often with great emotion, the types of teaching approaches and curriculum designs that can best accomplish the educational objectives of society. The conflict between those who support a traditional approach to education and those who support what has been labeled "progressive education" continues into the twenty-first century. This crucial debate will be the topic of the next chapter.

NOTES

1. "No Child Left Behind," *Education Week*, www.edweek.org/context/topics/issuespage.cfm?id=59 (accessed 14 September 2004), 1–3.

2. Robert J. Sternberg, "Good Intentions, Bad Results: A Dozen Reasons Why the No Child Left Behind Act is Failing," *Education Week*, 27 October 2004, www.edweek.org/ew/articles/2–4/10/27/09sternberg.h24.html?rale=14RcsgF70mP (accessed 27 October 2004), 1–3.

3. Nel Noddings, "Rethinking a Bad Law," *Education Week*, 23 February 2005 www.edweek.org/ew/articles/2005/02/23/24noddings.h24.html?rale=14RcsgF70mPt, (accessed 26 February 2005), 1–2.

4. Erik W. Robelen, "Paige: It's Not Too Early to Call a School Law a Success," *Education Week*, 6 October 2004, www.edweek.org/ew/articles/2004/10/06/06paige.h24.html (accessed 20 October 2004), 1.

5. Debra Viadero, "Report: States See Test-Score Gains," *Education Week*, 20 October 2004, www.edweek.org/ew/articles/2004/10/20/08edtrust.h24.html (accessed 20 October 2004), 1.

6. Debra Viadero, "Fuller's Work Touches Off Controversy," *Education Week*, 20 October 2004, www.edweek.org/ew/articles/2004/10/20/08pace.h24.html (accessed 20 October 2004), 1.

7. Sam Dillon, "Report Faults Bush Initiative on Education," *New York Times*, 24 February 2005, www.nytimes.com/2005/02/24/education/24child.html (accessed 26 February 2005), 1.

8. Kathleen Kennedy Manzo, "NCLB Reading Target to Be Missed, Study Says," *Education Week*, 16 December 2004, www.edweek.org/ew/articles/2004/12/16rand_webh24.html (accessed 16 December 2004), 1.

9. Alfie Kohn, "Joyless Endeavors," *Education Week*, 1 November 2004, www.edweek.org/tm/articles/2004/11/01/03view,h16,html?rale=14RcsgF70mPtCas (accessed 19 November 2004), 1.

10. Michelle R. Davis and Sean Cavanagh, "Bush to Seek Accountability in High School," at *Education Week*, 8 September 2004, www.edweek.org/ew/articles/2004/09/08/02gop.h24.html (accessed 20 November 2004), 1.

11. Karen MacPherson, "Odd allies oppose Bush education plan," *Post Gazette*, 13 February 2005, www.post-gazette.com/pg/05044/456387.stm (accessed 18 February 2005), 1.

12. CNN, "Bush denounces paying commentators," 26 January 2005, www.cnn.com/2005/ALLPOLITICS/01/26/bush.paidpundits.reut/index.html (accessed 27 January 2005), 1.

13. Sam Dillon, "New U.S. Secretary Showing Flexibility on 'No Child' Act," *New York Times*, 14 February 2005, www.nytimes.com/2005/02/14/politics/14educ.html (accessed 2 February 2005), 1–2.

14. Lynn Olson, "Taking Root," *Education Week*, 8 December 2004, www.edweek.org/ew/articles/2004/12/08/15nclb-1.h24.html (accessed 16 December 2004), 1–2.

15. Olson, "Taking Root," 6.

16. Richard Rothstein, "The Limits of Testing," *American School Board Journal*, January/February 2005, 34.

17. Rothstein, "The Limits of Testing," 37.

18. "Instructors say social studies suffering because of No Child Left Behind Act," National News Archives, 22 January 2005, www.nasspcms.principals.org/s_nassp/sec_Illumen.asp?CID=391&DID=47311&XMLD (accessed 7 February 2005), 1.

19. Lawrence A. Cremin, ed., *The Republic and the School: Horace Mann on the Education of Free Men* (New York: Bureau of Publications, Teachers College, Columbia University, 1957), 78.

15

THE DEBATE

At least since the work of John Dewey began to influence educational thinking at the beginning of the twentieth century, we have had a spirited debate in the United States about the way students learn and how teachers should teach. One could also make a case that such discussions were taking place during the lifetime of Horace Mann as he attempted to influence teaching methods in the schools in Massachusetts. Despite the fact that he and other nineteenth-century educators did attempt to modify how teachers approached their work, it was not until John Dewey helped launch what has been labeled the progressive education movement that educational thinking in this country became so divided.

This ongoing debate was described by David J. Ferrero in a recent article in *Educational Leadership* when he wrote:

> In fact, education's fiercest and most intractable conflicts have stemmed from differences in philosophy. Take the 100 Year's War between "progressives" and "traditionalists." To oversimplify an already oversimplified dichotomy, progressives incline toward pedagogical approaches that start with student interest and emphasize hands-on engagement with the physical and social environments, whereas traditionalists tend to start with pre-existing canons of inquiry and knowledge and emphasize ideas and concepts mediated through words and symbols.[1]

Almost all teachers, either knowingly or unknowingly, embraced the traditional philosophy until John Dewey and his disciples created what at least appeared to be a new way of approaching teaching and learning. As we began the twentieth century, classrooms were undoubtedly teacher-centered. The instructors at every level were thought of as dispensers of information. It was the role of the teacher to pass on to the students the knowledge and skills that society deemed appropriate for them to learn. There was a preordained curriculum, and formal lessons were prepared to ensure that students learned the required material. Traditional teaching did go beyond mere lecturing and often included classroom discussions or recitations. In an arithmetic or math class, it could also involve guided practice during which teachers moved about the classroom to help students. The traditional approach could also utilize visual aids and would not preclude the use of slides, movies, or even, today, PowerPoint presentations. The defining characteristic of the traditional approach to education is that it is teacher-centered and carefully structured.

John Dewey challenged this method when he established a laboratory school at the University of Chicago. At his school, "children were seen as socially active human beings eager to explore and gain control over their environment. By interacting with their world, learners confront both personal and social problems. Such problematic encounters stimulate children to use their intelligence to solve the difficulty and their knowledge in an active, instrumental manner."[2]

For Dewey, students should be taught to use the scientific method in problem solving. What would ideally happen in a progressive learning environment could be described as follows:

1. The learner is involved in a "genuine experience" that truly interests him or her.
2. Within this experience, the learner has a "genuine problem" that stimulates thinking.
3. The learner acquires the information needed to solve the problem.

4. The learner frames possible, tentative solutions that may solve the problem.
5. The learner tests the solutions by applying them to the problem. In this way, the learner constructs and validates his or her own knowledge.[3]

For progressive educators, teachers are primarily facilitators of learning. It is the job of an instructor to provide "hands-on" experiences that allow students to work on projects and to solve problems. For teachers embracing this philosophy, children learn best "by doing," not just being given information by a teacher. Students should be involved in problem solving when they are exposed to engaging issues that they are interested in learning about. As much as possible, educational experiences should grow out of student interest as opposed to a prepackaged curriculum prescribed by some far-off bureaucracy.

The progressives felt deeply that schools should provide a "liberating" environment "in which students were free to test all ideas, beliefs, and values."[4] John Dewey believed that "the educational center of gravity has been too long in the teacher, the textbook, anywhere and everywhere you please except in the immediate instincts and activities of the child himself." Educational historian Larry Cuban has written that "John Dewey believed that if schools were anchored in the whole child, in the social, intellectual, emotional, and physical development of a child, teaching . . . learning . . . and schools would be very different."[5]

Dewey's work has been used to justify many successful as well as unsuccessful innovations in education. Certainly there is a link between Dewey's work and such practices as cooperative learning, project-based learning, and student involvement in community activities as well as the use of field trips. Others would see Dewey's influence in the introduction of an increased reliance on laboratory experiments in science and even in the practice of whole language instruction. At the same time, others would point to such short-lived experiments as open classrooms and schools without walls as being in the progressive tradition. It is also true that Dewey's views grew and even changed somewhat during his long career and that those who attempted to follow his lead often went in directions that went beyond what Dewey himself could support. In addition, his writing is not always easy to understand and can easily be misinterpreted to justify questionable practices. In any case, his influence has generated the debate that has dominated educational discussion into the twenty-first century.

A new book written by journalist Robert Gray Holland is typical of the current strong feelings surrounding teaching and learning in the United States. He says in his book what many supporters of traditional education believe:

> Education has been susceptible to waves of goofy ideas down through the years. . . . They tend to emanate from high priced consultants, big companies with products to peddle, school bureaucracies, and the schools of education theorists with little or no connection to K–12 classroom reality.[6]

He goes on to blame most of what is wrong with public education on the teachers of future teachers in our college education programs. For him, it is these college professors in their "ivory towers" who are peddling the notion that schoolteachers should be "facilitators of learning rather than transmitters of knowledge." He argues that these professors are at odds with parents who want their children "to acquire basic knowledge and skills, in orderly and well-disciplined classrooms." Holland points to a 1997 study done by the Public Agenda organization titled "Different Drummers: How Teachers of Teachers View Public Education." The study turned up a "staggering" disconnection between the professors' view of education and the opinions held by parents, teachers, students, and civic leaders. Seventy-nine percent of the professors believed that the public's ideas about learning were "outmoded and mistaken."[7]

Other critics of current applications of progressive education thought are just as vehement. In a review of the book *The Promise and Failure of Progressive Education* by Norman Dale Norris, Sheila L. Macrine refers to the author's descriptions of educational programs that are gross misapplications of Dewey's work. Norris suggests that progressive education has become a caricature of what it was intended to be.[8]

Each decade of the twentieth century has seen new critics of the ideas of John Dewey. Such people as William Bagley in the 1930s, Arthur Bestor in the 1950s, and William Bennett in the 1990s have written about how Dewey's ideas were weakening the primary objectives of schools. For the many opponents of progressivism, schools should have as their primary function teaching the "basic skills of reading, writing, and arithmetic, and the fundamental intellectual disciplines of English and foreign languages, history, mathematics, and science." Anything else would dilute the school's primary mission.[9]

Even though his critics have been many, Dewey's approach to education will always have its defenders. Typical would be the current critic of the "back to basics" approach, John Holt, who has written:

> Behind much of what we do in school lie some ideas that could be expressed roughly as follows: (1) Of the vast body of human knowledge, there are certain bits and pieces that can be called essential. . . ; (2) the extent to which a person can be considered educated . . . depends on the amount of this essential knowledge that he carries about with him; (3) it is the duty of schools, therefore, to get as much of this essential knowledge as possible into the minds of children. . . . These ideas are absurd and harmful nonsense. . . . Children quickly forget all but a small part of what they learn in school. It is of no use or interest to them; they do not want, or expect, or even intend to remember it. The only difference between bad and good students in this respect is that bad students forget right away while the good students are careful to wait until after the exam.[10]

Another more contemporary writer who embraces the objectives of progressive education is Alfie Kohn, who believes that to be well educated means more than "knowing a lot of things." He is convinced that Dewey was right when he reminded his readers "that the goal of education is more education. To be well educated, then, is to have the desire as well as the means to make sure that learning never ends."[11] Kohn goes on to support Dewey's approach to education, suggesting:

> The best kind of teaching takes its cue from the understanding that people are active learners. In such a classroom, students are constantly making decisions, becoming participants in their own education. Each is part of a community of learners, coming to understand ideas from the inside out with one another's help. They still acquire facts and skills, but in a context, and for a purpose. Their questions drive the curriculum. Learning to think like scientists and historians matters more than memorizing lists of definitions and dates.[12]

E. D. Hirsch, who labels himself a political liberal but an educational conservative, disagrees with Dewey. He has written an article in which he asks the question, "Is there an available alternative to today's failed progressive education?" His answer is that the alternative is what he calls knowledge-based education. He goes on to charge that compared to the education received by many Europeans and Asians, most American children are "underprivileged."[13]

The debate between those who support the ideas of John Dewey and those who believe them to be subversive to the fundamental purposes of education will continue. Even so, one cannot question the fact that the principles and practices of progressive educational thought have influenced not only our teacher education programs but to a lesser degree what actually goes on in public school classrooms. Anyone wishing to read more deeply about the division among educators in our country can use this list of books, which was published in a recent *Educational Leadership* issue.

Traditionalist
- Mortimer J. Adler, *The Paideia Proposal* (Macmillan, 1982)
- Jacques Barzun, *A Jacques Barzun Reader* (HarperCollins, 2001)
- Earl Shorris, *Riches for the Poor* (W.W. Norton & Company, 2000)
- E. D. Hirsch Jr., *Cultural Literacy* (Vintage, 1988)
- Lisa Delpit, *Other People's Children* (New Press, 1996)
- William J. Bennett, *Curriculum for American Students* (Diane Publishing Company, 1988)

Progressive

- Deborah Meier, *The Power of Their Ideas* (Beacon Press, 1996)
- Theodore R. Sizer, *Horace's School* (Mariner Books, 1997)
- Eliot Levine, *One Kid at a Time* (Teachers College Press, 2001)
- Paulo Freire, *Pedagogy of the Oppressed* (Continuum International Publishing Group; 30th Anniversary edition, 2000)
- George S. Counts, *Dare the School Build a New Social Order?* (Southern Illinois University Press, 1978)
- David Stern et al., *Career Academies* (Jossey-Bass, 1992)[14]

Just as judges and historians often study the views of the Founding Fathers in attempting to seek guidance on contemporary constitutional issues, today's educators could perhaps benefit by considering the views of an individual who has been labeled the "father of the public schools." It is difficult to pinpoint exactly what position Horace Mann would take in the heated dialogue between traditionalists and progressives. In support of the traditionalist point of view, Mann was prepared to give to the local superintendent, along with the state, the power to develop the curriculum to be used in the schools of Massachusetts. He believed that all curricular offerings and teacher materials should be standardized and that students should be grouped by age into "graded schools."[15] Yet his thoughts about teaching methods might fit more comfortably with those of the progressives. He respected teaching as a very profound and complex activity, calling it "the most difficult of all arts, and the profoundest of all sciences."[16]

Horace Mann believed "that knowledge cannot be poured into a child's mind, like a fluid from one vessel to another . . . there must be a conscious effort on his part."[17] He argued in his second report to the Massachusetts Board of Education:

> Children, who spend six months in learning the alphabet, will, on the playground in single half day or moonlight evening, learn the intricacies of a game or sport,—where to stand, when to run, what to say, how to count, and what are the laws and the ethics of the game;—the whole requiring more intellectual effort than would suffice to learn half a dozen alphabets . . . the process of learning words and letters

is toilsome and progress will be slow, unless a motive is inspired before instruction is attempted.[18]

Horace Mann believed that motivation to learn was essential and that students would obviously work harder if they truly were interested in the subject. In order to provide this motivation, he was convinced that a variety of teaching techniques are essential. Teachers must have

> a knowledge of methods and processes. These are indefinitely various . . . he who is apt to teach is acquainted, not only with common methods for common minds but with peculiar methods for pupils of peculiar dispositions and temperaments; and he is acquainted with the principles of all methods, whereby he can vary his plan, according to any differences of circumstances.[19]

Perhaps the best evidence as to Mann's views on teaching can be seen in the way he taught his own classes after he became the president of Antioch College. One of his students, Henry Clay Badger, kept a diary during his years as a student at Antioch. He noted that Horace Mann gave to students "special lessons" that were assigned to "special pupils, giving each some question to pursue at leisure and upon which to prepare a paper to be read to the whole class."[20] For his pupil Badger, what was exciting about Mann's teaching was "the impetus with which his mind smote our minds." He "kindled a heat of enthusiasm."[21] There is no question that Horace Mann, in his own teaching, was doing more than passing on knowledge to his students. The fact is that he believed that "rote learning of names and rules was neither effective nor desirable."[22]

It would seem clear to anyone examining the works of Horace Mann that he would have felt somewhat comfortable with many of the progressive educators of the twentieth century. During his own lifetime, he was actively challenging the traditional approaches to education. Still, he was certainly not ready to throw away formal curriculums and textbooks. If he were participating in our current educational dialogue, he most likely would have been somewhere near the middle or slightly left of center of the two points of view. He believed that there are certain things that society must teach its young and that decisions on curriculum should not be left to the individual interest of either a single teacher or a single student. While those who have the responsibility and authority should have the power to create what we call today "standards," the decision as to how these standards are to be imparted to students should be left to a trained teacher. It is also likely that he would be concerned if a prescribed and rigid system of testing is making it difficult or impossible for teachers to have the necessary latitude to do their job and to teach creatively. There is certainly a chance that Horace Mann would join the fight to alter the system of "high-stakes" testing and accountability that we have created. His goal most likely would be to find an appropriate balance between the right of society to establish educational objectives and the prerogatives of a professional teacher to determine the methods for reaching these established curriculum standards.

Unfortunately, neither of these objectives can be adequately met if society does not provide schools that give an equal educational opportunity to all children. Horace Mann's vision for publicly supported schools was premised on the assumption that these schools would offer an equal educational opportunity for all children. Many would argue that our present approach for funding schools has been unsuccessful in reaching this goal. It is to the question of school funding to which we must now turn.

NOTES

1. David J. Ferrero, "Pathways to Reform: Start with Values," *Educational Leadership* 62, no. 5 (February 2005): 10.

2. Sandra Rosenthal, "Democracy and Education: A Deweyan Approach," *Educational Theory*, Fall 1993, 377–89.

3. John Dewey, *Democracy and Education* (New York: Macmillan, 1916), 192.

4. Allan C. Ornstein and Daniel U. Levine, *Foundations of Education* (Boston: Houghton Mifflin, 2006), 145.

5. Sarah Mondale and Sarah B. Patton, eds., *School: The Story of American Public Education* (Boston: Beacon Press, 2001), 76–77.

6. Robert Gray Holland, *To Build a Better Teacher* (Westport, CT: Praeger, 2004), xiii.

7. Holland, *Better Teacher*, xvi–xvii.

8. Sheila L. Macrine, "The Promise and Failure of Progressive Education," *TC Record*, http://tcrecord.frameworkers.com/Content.asp?ContentID=11715, (accessed 16 February 2005), 1.

9. Gerald L. Gutek, *Historical and Philosophical Foundations of Education* (Upper Saddle River, NJ: Pearson, 2005), 349.

10. Jack J. Nelson, Stuart B. Palonsky, and Mary Rose McCarthy, *Critical Issues in Education: Dialogues and Dialectics* (Boston: McGraw-Hill, 2004), 235.

11. Alfie Kohn, "What Does It Mean to Be Well Educated?" *Beacon*, www.beacon.org/k-12/june2004/kohn_chap1.html, (accessed 16 February 2005), 7.

12. Alfie Kohn, "A LOOK AT . . . Getting Back to Basics: First Lesson: Unlearn How We Learned," *Washington Post*, 10 October 1999, www.alfiekohn.org/teaching/alagbtb.htm (accessed 14 March 2005), 3.

13. E. D. Hirsch, "Why Traditional Education is More Progressive," *American Enterprise* www.taemag.com/issues/articleid.16209/article_detail.asp (accessed 14 March 2005), 6

14. Ferrero, "Pathways to Reform: Start with Values," *Educational Leadership*, 14.

15. L. Glenn Smith and Joan K. Smith, *Lives in Education* (New York: St. Martin's Press, 1994), 247.

16. Joy Elmer Morgan, *Horace Mann: His Ideas and Ideals*, (Washington, D.C.: National Home Library Foundation, 1936), 135.

17. Lawrence A. Cremin, ed., *The Republic and the School: Horace Mann on the Education of Free Men* (New York: Bureau of Publications, Teachers College, Columbia University, 1957), 37.

18. Cremin, *Republic and the School*, 38–39.

19. "Motivational Quotes for Teachers," http://www.pitt.edu/~poole/ARCHIVE#.HTML (accessed 14 March 2005), 2.

20. Louise Hall Tharpe, *Until Victory: Horace Mann and Mary Peabody* (Boston: Little, Brown and Company, 1953), 279–80.

21. Tharpe, *Until Victory*, 279–80.

22. Robert Badolato, The Educational Theory of Horace Mann," www.newfoundations.com/GALLERY/Mann.html (accessed 27 September 2004), 2.

16

THE FINANCIAL
DILEMMA

Although they vary from year to year, state to state, and between
districts in the same state, the sources of public school financing currently break down approximately as follows:

- State government—49.7 percent
- Local government—43 percent
- Federal government—7.3 percent[1]

States are playing a growing role in financing public schools as
they attempt to develop formulas that balance the inequities in
funding caused by the differences in the ability of local districts to
raise money through property taxes. To provide the state portion of
the school revenues, governors and legislatures have created a variety of taxes and other revenue sources. Most important are the state
income taxes and sales taxes. Some states raise significant amounts
of money with high taxes on so-called luxury items such as tobacco
and alcohol products. Others resort to an array of fees in such areas
as car registrations and licenses. A number of states have sought to
raise money for schools by using lotteries and even gambling casinos
as an income source. As the demands on states created by a significant number of legal challenges to their school aid formulas increase, legislators will undoubtedly struggle to find new sources of
income to support schools.

At the local level, almost all of this income is derived from property taxes. By far, the most important advantage of this source of income is that it is easy to administer at the local level. Most often it is the responsibility of a local government other than the school district to assess the value of all property in its jurisdiction. During the annual budget process, the school board first determines how much money must be raised from the local property tax. Using local assessment rolls, district officials then set a tax rate per 1,000 on assessed property. If the tax rate is set at twenty dollars per 1,000, the owners of a home assessed for $100,000 would pay $2,000 in school taxes. The money is collected locally and delinquent taxpayers are assessed late fees; and if taxes go unpaid for a prolonged period, the local government can eventually take over the property.

While the ease in administering and collecting property taxes is the primary advantage, there are a number of problems associated with such a tax. First and foremost is the fact that property-poor districts cannot raise money as easily as more affluent districts because their assessments are lower and because the residents and often the businesses cannot easily absorb increases in their property tax. In affluent suburban districts, not only is it easier to raise taxes on people's homes, but they often have malls and other businesses that are highly taxed. City districts, which have lost numerous people and businesses to the suburbs, and rural areas dominated by farms are especially disadvantaged by the use of property taxes to fund schools. With less than a third of the taxpayers having children in the public schools, it is increasingly difficult, especially in poorer districts, to gain support for property tax increases. As the population of the nation ages, we also have more and more senior citizens on fixed incomes. Increases in school budgets as well as in property assessments can make it difficult for less affluent retirees to pay their school taxes each year.

Other critics question the fairness of the property tax system. With a housing market that can frequently change in a community, it is extremely difficult even for the most conscientious assessor to gauge the exact retail value of each and every property in a municipality. Theoretically, the assessment on one's property represents what it could be sold for at that particular time. Despite the fact that assessors offer citizens a grievance procedure, there are residents in every district who are unhappy with the assessment system. Although qualifications vary from district to district, exemptions from paying property taxes are very frequent. Included may be all government buildings, military bases, hospitals, churches, and colleges among other institutions. Special deductions in property taxes are sometimes granted to farmers, senior citizens, and veterans. In order to encourage economic growth in the area, some municipalities offer tax reductions to businesses that are willing to move into the community. All of these exceptions reduce the tax base and place more burdens on homeowners and businesses. Because of the resistance of local taxpayers to increases in property taxes, added pressure has been placed on state governments and now the federal government to make a larger contribution to funding schools.

The third source of income for financing schools is the federal government. Beginning with the passage of the Elementary and Secondary Education Act in 1965, the federal government has become involved in helping to fund selected programs in the public schools. Although billions of federal dollars have been spent on public education, the percentage of federal funding of schools has never risen above 10 percent. The primary source of aid has been Title I of the Elementary and Secondary Education Act, which provides school districts with money to establish remedial reading and math programs for disadvantaged students. The No Child Left Behind Act is actually a reauthorization of this legislation that places major new federal mandates on school districts if they are to continue collecting Title I money. In addition, the federal government has provided funding for preschool Head Start programs and special education programs, as well as the school lunch program. These are just a few of the areas that have been chosen as priorities by Congress and the president. There are numerous smaller grants available, many of which are given competitively based on applications submitted by local districts.

Despite the fact that schools are utilizing revenue from the federal and state governments as well as from local sources, the present system is not functioning as well as it might. The main problem is that state and federal aid does not balance the inequities between those school districts that can easily raise money from local property taxes and those that, because of poverty and low property values, cannot raise the necessary funds at the local level. Numerous lawsuits at the state level have been filed by districts or by groups of districts, claiming that the state is not adequately providing for the students in their district. Starting in 1973, there have been cases that have challenged the aid formulas of various states. Such lawsuits have been brought in thirty different states, most of them claiming discrimination based on race or social class. The critics of the current system of financing schools would claim that the unequal educational opportunity resulting from unfair funding of public schools is responsible for a "growing economic stratification in society at large."[2] Although in a number of the cases courts have been able to force some reform of the funding systems, the results thus far were summarized by Stan Karp when he wrote that

> court decisions, in themselves, have been insufficient to ensure equity for several reasons. While glaring disparities in school funding have occasionally persuaded the Courts to order reform, it has been almost impossible to prevent Governors and state legislators from evading or limiting the impact of the court orders. Restrained by separation-of-powers concerns and the prevailing conservative political climate, Courts have generally given states wide latitude to proceed with the half-measures and "good faith" efforts, sometimes promising further review if they prove inadequate.[3]

A recent study has shown that despite the court challenges, inequities in spending between more affluent districts and poor districts are growing. In a *New York Times* article headlined "Wider Gap Found Between Wealthy and Poor Schools," writer Greg Winter cites a new report that shows that in 2002, "high poverty districts typically received $868 more per student" from state and federal sources than their counterparts that had relatively few poor children. "As recently as 2000, the gap was down to $728." The same article raises the point that educating poor children is actually much more expensive than working with children from more affluent homes. The report claims that "districts with large proportions of poor students would have needed $1,350 more per child than they received in 2002 to achieve parity."[4]

If one accepts the premise that it costs more to educate poor children, then thirty-six states have funding gaps. Even if this concept is discounted, there are still twenty-five states where districts are spending more per pupil in affluent districts.[5] Large states, including New York, Virginia, and Texas, are involved in legal controversies over their formulas for state aid to education. New York, Illinois, and Virginia are the states with the largest gaps in spending, with students in the affluent districts receiving more than $2,000 per pupil than those from poor districts.[6]

There are those who feel that additional money for public schools will make little difference in their academic achievement, but most educators would agree with the conclusion of Amy M. Azzam, who wrote in *Educational Leadership* that "closing the achievement gap is a familiar theme these days. But lurking behind the achievement gap is another contentious issue: funding. Excellence in education doesn't come without a price tag."[7]

Thus as a nation, we find ourselves with both a funding gap and an achievement gap between children attending schools in poorer communities and those who live in affluent districts. Because of housing patterns, it is African American and Hispanic children who are most often found attending schools that are less well-off. The question then becomes, how can we as a nation establish an equal educational opportunity for all children given our method of financing schools and the current demographics of our nation?

In an article published in *Phi Delta Kappan,* titled "The New Common School," Charles L. Glenn, the director of equal educational opportunity for the Massachusetts Department of Education, returns to the vision of Horace Mann in an attempt to put forward what he feels should be the direction of our public schools. He quotes Horace Mann's view that "the distinction of rich and poor, high and low, patrician and plebian, has no place under our institutions," and he goes on to note that it was Mann's belief that all children in a locality would attend school together. For Horace Mann, this meant that poor children and minority children would have an equal opportunity to succeed and that all students would learn the same lessons and be treated with respect and affection by their teachers. Glenn argues that because we are increasingly seeing students attending schools with others in their own social class, Mann's vision must be altered. He states that "public schools can no longer claim to be the common schools that Mann envisioned. Indeed, a good case has been made that the most exclusive schools in America today are not private schools but public schools in affluent suburbs." Because of the housing patterns that have evolved in many of our districts, the author believes that the best way to mix students is to develop a true choice system. He lists the following pedagogical reasons for instituting schools of choice:

- Students have different needs and strengths; they think and learn in different ways.
- Schools are more effective and take a more coherent approach to instruction when their educational mission is clear.
- Students seem to learn more in schools and programs that they and their parents have chosen.[8]

Needless to say, school choice has become a popular alternative in many large districts during the past two decades. It is not really a practical option for the smaller rural and suburban districts unless we reorganize and consolidate many of these schools. To date, there is not a great deal of evidence that magnet schools, charter schools, or experimental voucher systems are solving either the achievement gap or the funding gap between rich and poor school districts. Neither, it would seem, is the choice option compatible with Horace Mann's vision for the public schools. Where there is choice, there is a variety of educational objectives. The magnet school for the arts has different goals than a vocational high school. Horace Mann was clear on what should be the focus for all common schools. He believed that along with teaching the basic skills, music, science, and physical education, it was imperative that schools concentrate on creating good people who would be able to effectively participate in our capitalistic economy and democratic governmental system. In Mann's own words:

The theory of our laws and institutions undoubtedly is, first, that in every district of every town of the Commonwealth, there should be a free district school, sufficiently safe, and sufficiently good, for all the children within its territory, where they may be well instructed in the rudiments of knowledge, formed to the propriety of demeanor, and imbued with the principles of duty.[9]

Since he constantly fought for additional local and state funding for schools, it seems that Horace Mann would have agreed that underfunded schools in poor districts is a problem that requires the immediate attention of governments at all levels. In addition, it is probable that he, like most contemporary educators, would accept the fact that these schools in poor areas need additional funding and attention. By giving students in poorer neighborhoods special help, he might well have felt that we could begin to erase some of the growing gap between rich and poor in this country. Although Horace Mann was very far from being a socialist, one can at least conjecture that he would be in the forefront for general reform measures to help lower- and middle-class Americans. He was concerned in his own time about the growing economic differences between the owners of the new industries and the working class. He would also be alarmed today by the effects of the escalating compensation for our current CEOs compared to the wages being paid to average workers in their companies. It is hard to believe that he would not be a supporter of higher minimum wages, tax reductions for the working poor rather than the rich, and other programs that would lift families with poor children out of poverty.

During his period of leadership in Massachusetts, Mann looked to the state government to assist local communities in paying for their schools. Whether his time in Washington as a congressman and lecturing throughout the United States would have caused him to eventually turn to the federal government for funding, we cannot know. What is clear is what he believed:

Wealthy people have a special responsibility in providing public education. Those who had prospered, . . . were guardians or stewards of wealth. In addition, their support of public education would create industrious men and women who would obey the law, be diligent in their work, and add to the state's economy. Thus tax support of public education was actually an investment that would yield high dividends in the form of public safety, progress, and prosperity . . . the common school would be a great social equalizer, giving children from lower socioeconomic classes the skills and knowledge to acquire better jobs and upward mobility.[10]

The eternal optimist, Mann most likely would conclude today that we have the necessary wealth and knowledge to provide public schools, which can be "a great equalizer of opportunity."[11] If our schools are truly to function the way Horace Mann envisioned, our nation must accept as a national priority the need to provide equal educational opportunities for all children. Beyond this, we will need to accept the reality that schools in our poorer neighborhoods need extra attention and money. Causing this to happen will not be easy. Timothy A. Hacsi has framed our national challenge with these words:

> Even if the evidence were to become crystal clear about how to build superb schools in every school district, it would be an extraordinarily difficult thing to do, in part because the financing of schools would remain, fundamentally, a political issue. To increase school budgets, taxes have to be increased somewhere; should they be local property taxes, or state sales or income taxes, or should the federal government greatly increase its contribution? How can the public—most of which does not have children of school age—be convinced that more money should go to schools rather than their own direct needs? Perhaps the first step is a wider recognition by politicians and citizens that, while money will not automatically make a difference, it is a necessary component of any true educational reform, especially when it comes to our most troubled schools.[12]

Thus far, this book has been considering how Horace Mann might have reacted today to the major issues confronting public schools. Having done this, it now seems appropriate to attempt not only to summarize Mann's vision for the public schools, but to suggest how that vision might be helpful as we enter the twenty-first century. This will be the task that is undertaken in the final chapter.

NOTES

1. David Miller Sadker and Myra Pollack Sadker, *Teachers, Schools, and Society* (Boston: McGraw-Hill, 2005), 362.

2. Stan Karp, "Money, Schools, and Courts," *Z Magazine*, December 1995, www.geocities.com/Athens/Cyprus/6547/money.html (accessed 6 February 2004), 1.

3. Karp, "Money, Schools, and Courts," 2.

4. Greg Winter, "Wider Gap Found Between Wealthy and Poor Schools," *New York Times*, 6 October 2004, www.nytimes.com/2004/10/06/education/06gap.html (accessed 7 October 2004), 1.

5. Joetta L. Sack, "Aid Disparities in Needy Schools Seen as Rising," *Education Week*, 13 October 2004, www.edweek.org/ew/articles/2004/10/13/07finance.h24.html?rale=14RcsgF70mPt (accessed 15 October 2004), 1.

6. Christina A. Samuels, "Virginia Faulted for Funding Gap Between Rich, Poor Schools," *Washington Post*, 6 October 2004, www.washingtonpost.com/wp-dyn/articles/A9699-2004Oct5.html (accessed 6 October 2004), 1.

7. Amy M. Azzam, "The Funding Gap," *Educational Leadership* 62, no. 5 (February 2005): 93.

8. Charles L. Glenn, "The New Common School," *Phi Delta Kappan*, December 1987, 1–3.

9. Gerald L. Gutek, *Historical and Philosophical Foundations of Education* (Upper Saddle River, NJ: Pearson, 2005), 224.

10. Allan C. Ornstein and Daniel U. Levine, *Foundations of Education* (Boston: Houghton Mifflin, 2006), 170.

11. Robert Badolato, "The Educational Theory of Horace Mann," www.newfoundations.com/GALLERY/Mann.html (accessed 27 September 2004), 3.

12. Timothy A. Hacsi, *Children as Pawns* (Cambridge, MA: Harvard University Press, 2002), 203.

THE MANN PLAN

Much of what has happened with public schools since his death would be pleasing to Horace Mann. The fact that we now have free tax-supported schools in every community and that they enroll at least 90 percent of the school-age children would be a source of great pride to him and to his fellow pioneers in the public school movement. He would be surprised and gratified by the fact that public education is now in place for secondary students as well as those in the elementary grades. In addition, he would undoubtedly be thrilled by the fact that there are compulsory attendance laws in every state. Given the condition of school buildings during his life-time, Horace Mann could not help but be impressed by the build-ings that now house many of our finest public schools.

The education programs currently preparing teachers in our pri-vate and public colleges go far beyond the meager instruction avail-able in the normal schools established by Horace Mann. He would be pleased with the present requirements for teacher certification and would applaud the states and districts that have ongoing pro-fessional growth programs for their teachers. In regard to the cur-riculum being taught in our public schools, Mann would be sup-portive of the current requirements in language arts, mathematics, science, physical education, health, and music.

There is little question that he would approve as well of the part-nership that has developed between local and state governments in financing and managing the schools. It is doubtful that after his service in Congress, Horace Mann would have quarreled with the fact that the federal government has also become a partner in supporting public education. The centralization of smaller districts into larger districts is a trend that is also in keeping with his own programs in Massachusetts. Considering all this, Horace Mann could not help but be impressed by the way his vision of free, tax-supported schools has prospered.

That being said, he would also most likely be prepared to take issue with a number of developments in our school systems. Perhaps most important would be the fact that educational opportunities for children are currently far different depending on the wealth of the school district. If he were to travel from school to school today as he did in Massachusetts during his lifetime, he would find suburban schools with better libraries, lower class sizes, better-prepared teachers, more attractive buildings, and better-equipped classrooms. A few miles away, he might find overcrowded urban schools with deteriorating buildings and a significant number of uncertified teachers. In some of the rural areas, there would also be stark differences between the schools available to these children and the schools located in the nearby suburbs. Such differences would be contrary to Mann's vision of providing excellent schools for all children whatever their race or social class.

In regard to the current curriculums being offered, he would be concerned that we are doing too little to achieve what, for him, were the two major objectives of public schools. Mann believed that it is the role of the school to develop virtuous people who are prepared to contribute to our economy and to our democratic system. While he would support the efforts of some districts to include character education programs and experiences in participating in local government, he would undoubtedly argue that such programs should become central to the curriculum and not be thought of as add-ons. He thought that the common school should and could improve society by ensuring that children were imbued with those traits of character that would lead to a more peaceful and prosperous society and world. Schools need to be a training ground for life and not just a place where children learn to read and write.

At least for the early grades, Horace Mann would be worried about our current emphasis on high-stakes testing. If these tests are allowed to become the paramount objective of education, the focus of the public schools would become too narrow to meet the high expectations for schools envisioned by Horace Mann. He would caution our current leaders as to what might occur because of the No Child Left Behind law. Like many of our current critics, he would worry about the new emphasis on test results and how those subjects chosen for standardized testing would force a de-emphasis on other objectives of the school.

Although it is hard to know, he might well also question our extensive extracurricular programs. He would undoubtedly see the potential value of giving students the opportunity to participate in student councils, school newspapers, and debate clubs. On the other hand, he might be amazed that students are spending twenty hours each week playing on an interscholastic athletic team, while those same teenagers are only doing homework for four hours a week.

It is also probable that Horace Mann would have been troubled by the current trend toward school choice. This would be especially true in the case of voucher plans, which give equal funding to religious-based schools. He would see this as being just the opposite of what he was trying to establish with the common schools. While Horace Mann did not suggest that private religious schools should be closed, he did seek to create free public schools that were as good as or better than any private school. His dream was to bring into these schools children from all religious backgrounds, races, and social classes. In such a school, all children would have an equal opportunity to succeed, and at the same time, they would learn to respect people who were different than themselves. If he were to look at the current evidence regarding school choice programs, he might well conclude that these experiments have yet to prove that they will ever solve our segregation problems or the academic gap that exists between white and Asian-American children and children from African American or Hispanic families.[1]

At the same time, he could not help but worry about the current segregation of our society caused by housing patterns. Like our current political and education leaders, he would be perplexed about how we can best create school systems that bring together in the same classrooms a mixture of races, religions, and social classes. Our present school district pattern continues to be based on the assumption that children will attend their neighborhood public schools. Unfortunately, the way our housing patterns have developed, our schools have become more segregated. This has caused urban school systems to be primarily made up of minority students, while our suburban and rural districts have mainly Caucasian children.

Given this threat to his vision, we can only guess what Horace Mann might have proposed. During his lifetime, he was already worried about the growing gap between laborers and employers. He was hoping that the common school would provide to all graduates the ability to make a decent living and the ambition to better themselves. The current pattern that characterizes the distribution of income in the United States would be a major concern to Horace Mann. Because it now appears that many government policies have encouraged larger differences between the "haves" and the "have-nots," it is probable that Mann would have sought ways to reduce these differences. If he were representing his state in Congress today, it is hard to believe that he would not be supporting efforts to raise the minimum wage and to reduce taxes for the poor. At the same time, he would likely believe that tax reductions for the rich, whether they are on income, capital gains, or inheritances, would be detrimental to society.

Now that the federal government has become a major player in public education, Horace Mann would probably be supportive of national programs designed to help poor school districts. He certainly would have supported college scholarship programs for children from poor families. It can be assumed that he also would be sympathetic to any state or local initiatives that would help poor people better their economic condition. This feeling would be strengthened if he were to read some of the descriptions of the current effects of poverty on our students. In an article discussing the impact of poverty on education, titled "Education Vital Signs 2005," it is pointed out:

> No matter how you define it, poverty is rising-and taking a toll on kids . . . as a group, poor children do not perform as well as middle-class students because of the social and economic conditions under which they live. The solution to their predicament cannot be found in education policy alone, but through a broader effort to address other critical needs, such as jobs, housing, and health care.[2]

For Horace Mann, the best way for society to deal with poverty was through education. He believed that public education "does better than to disarm the poor of their hostility towards the rich; it prevents being poor."[3]

For his vision of the public schools to function effectively, steps would need to be taken to bring about more integrated neighborhoods. With this in mind, it is likely that he would support efforts to lure middle-class white families back into our cities and to stem the tide of "white flight" to the suburbs and rural areas. Until such policies are successful in bringing about more integrated neighborhood schools, I believe that Horace Mann would not oppose voluntary urban-suburban arrangements that allow students to attend schools outside of their neighborhood. For the same reason, he might be open to efforts to redraw school district boundary lines to create a better racial balance.

At the same time, as an educator, congressman, or college president, it is probably true that Horace Mann would have been in the forefront in the effort to establish school funding formulas that allow schools in poorer areas to provide programs equal to those offered in affluent school districts. As a sensitive educator and legislator, he might well have gone further to support additional funds for those schools with a larger-than-average percentage of students designated as in need of special education or in need of additional help in the English language.

Of all of the concerns he might have about our current schools, the most important one for Horace Mann would be that we include in our current curriculums some type of character and citizenship education. Even more than in his own lifetime, he would see the need for such programs. Given the problems in our schools with the use of alcohol, drugs, and potential violence, he would be more than ever supportive of the need to teach students how to live a virtuous life. A cursory look at the percentage of young voters would also cause him to seek to redouble the efforts of schools in teaching the responsibilities of citizenship. The importance of such efforts as part of his vision for the common schools cannot be overemphasized. Despite the current emphasis on multicultural education, Horace Mann would urge that there be a concerted effort to emphasize that whatever a student's background, he or she is first and foremost an American citizen. While students could certainly be proud of their cultural ancestry, he would argue that it is essential to try to use the school to bring children together and to give them a common education.

Horace Mann would also be very interested in our current discussions in regard to the proper relationship between church and state. Most likely, he would applaud those laws and court decisions that have kept denominational religious training out of the public schools. Especially because of our growing religious diversity, he probably would not be upset with the current state of the law. A possible exception would be the restrictions on the use of the Bible in school and perhaps some of the limitations on nondenominational prayer. It is instructive that despite the criticisms of his religious convictions, Horace Mann said to his children while on his deathbed that "when you wish to know what to do, ask yourselves what Christ would have done in the same circumstances."[4]

Along with religion in schools, Horace Mann would be interested in the current trends related to vocational education and academic grouping. Any practice adopted by educators that divided students, especially younger children, into separate groups would concern him. The goal of the common school movement was to bring all children into a "common" classroom where they could all experience a "common" educational experience. To this extent, he would agree with the goals of the No Child Left Behind Act, which is attempting to maintain high academic standards for all children.

While he would have taken great interest in innovations that promised to lead to improved academic achievement for children, Horace Mann might have had some doubts about an overreliance on technology. For him, the role of the teacher as a model was central to the success of schools. Online courses that separate the student and the teacher would make such modeling more difficult. As a supporter of libraries and books, it would be hard to think of him, at least at this point in time, as a teacher who would like his research students to use only the Internet for their sources.

Horace Mann always believed that the teacher was central to the educational process. In this respect, he expected teachers to be role models for their students both in and out of the classroom. Some tactics currently used by teachers' unions would have disturbed him. His personal image of the perfect common school teacher would have been a totally committed, saintlike woman whose life revolved around her students. Seeing a teacher carrying a picket sign would not have fitted his image. A teacher drinking in a local bar would have been unacceptable to a man who sponsored legislation against the sale of alcoholic beverages. He also would have been opposed to the current practice of using lottery revenues to finance schools, given the fact that as a state legislator, he also sponsored laws opposing "traffic in lottery tickets."[5]

As the secretary to the Board of Education in Massachusetts, Horace Mann also tried to reform the practice of using corporal punishment in schools. He very much wanted schools to be places that children desired to attend. For him, creating a positive learning environment was essential. Today, he would be disappointed and alarmed at the security measures necessary in many of our schools. Closed-circuit surveillance cameras and armed security guards would have been contrary to his vision.

He would have also been concerned with many of our current large schools. During his lifetime he supported creating larger districts, but given our current difficulties, it is very possible that he would be urging smaller schools and smaller classes.

I don't believe that Horace Mann, a leader who never rested in his efforts to reform society, would be overwhelmed or pessimistic as a result of our current educational dilemmas. Although some of his ideas, which were formulated more than a century and a half ago, might be somewhat outdated, in the United States, most Americans continue to support his vision of a free and equal educational opportunity for all children. Perhaps more important than anything else we can learn from the life and works of Horace Mann is the example of his unceasing commitment to education as the most important way to improve society. It is easy for a nation to become so concerned about issues related to its economy and foreign policy that it neglects to focus on the institutions that will have the most effect on the future.

Horace Mann truly believed that "the common school is the greatest discovery ever made by man." While few would necessarily agree with this lofty ideal, most people in the United States are committed to the idea of free public schools. We can learn from Horace Mann that without a high level of commitment to providing equal educational opportunity for all children, this goal will never be reached. We need to be reminded of his conviction that it is the "absolute right" of every human being to have the opportunity for an education and that it is the "duty of every government to see that the means of that education are provided for all."[6] To do this, we must take to heart the words of Horace Mann when he said:

> Some eulogize our system of Popular Education, as though worthy to be universally admired and imitated. Others pronounce it, circumscribed in its action, and feeble, even when it acts. Let us waste no time in composing this strife. If good, let us improve it; if bad, let us reform it.[7]

Mann never questioned the fact that we could always reform and improve upon the status quo. In his final report to the Board of Education of Massachusetts, he wrote that "if we believe in our individual capacity for indefinite improvement, why should we doubt the capacity of the race for continued progress, as long as it dwells upon the earth?"[8]

One cannot help but admire the spirit of optimism and commitment displayed by Horace Mann. For him, making a difference was one of the most important aspects of a good life. In his final address to the students at Antioch College, he said, "be ashamed to die until you have had some victory for humanity."[9]

In conclusion, we return to the question raised by the title of this book, Is Horace Mann's vision of the public schools still relevant? There is little doubt that although many historical trends have affected the development of our public schools in America, they have become a vibrant and important aspect of our society. In many ways, they are a unique but imperfect American institution that continues to be a primary force in shaping our future. Even with their many imperfections, they remain a primary means for ensuring a brighter future. Horace Mann and his generation accomplished their goal of establishing free, tax-supported schools for every child. But there is still much to be done. It is up to future generations, including our own, to carry on their vision. To create excellent public schools in every community could truly be our "victory for humanity."

NOTES

1. Gerald W. Bracey, "The 13th Bracey Report on The Condition of Public Education," *Phi Delta Kappan*, October 2003, 148–64.

2. "Educational Vital Signs 2005," http://www.asbj.com/evs/05/poverty .html (accessed 29 March 2005), 1.

3. David W. Kirkpatrick, "A Contrarian View of Horace Mann," U.S. Freedom Foundation, http://www.freedomfoundation.us/horace_mann (accessed 17 March 2005), 1.

4. Mary Peabody Mann, *The Life and Works of Horace Mann* (Boston: Lee and Shepard, 1891), 553.

5. Joy Elmer Morgan, *Horace Mann, His Ideas and Ideals* (Washington, DC: The National Home Library Foundation, 1936), 12.

6. Lawrence A. Cremin, ed., *The Republic and the School: Horace Mann on the Education of Free Men* (New York: Bureau of Publications, Teachers College, Columbia University, 1957), 63.

7. Morgan, *Horace Mann, His Ideas and Ideals*, 49.

8. Morgan, *Horace Mann, His Ideas and Ideals*, 125.

9. Louise Hall Tharpe, *Until Victory: Horace Mann and Mary Peabody* (Boston: Little, Brown and Company, 1953), 310.

ABOUT THE AUTHOR

William Hayes has been a high school social studies teacher, department chair, assistant principal, and high school principal. From 1973 to 1994, he served as superintendent of schools for the Byron-Bergen Central School District, which is located eighteen miles west of Rochester, NY. During his career, he was an active member of the New York State Council of Superintendents, and he is the author of a council publication titled *The Superintendency: Thoughts for New Superintendents,* which is used to prepare new superintendents in New York State.

Hayes has also written a number of articles for various educational journals. After retiring from the superintendency he served as chair of the Teacher Education Division at Roberts Wesleyan College in Rochester, NY, until 2003. He currently remains a full-time teacher at Roberts Wesleyan. During the past six years he has written eight books, which have all been published by Scarecrow Education. They include *Real-Life Case Studies for School Administrators, Real-Life Case Studies for Teachers, So You Want to be a Superintendent?, So You Want to be a School Board Member?, Real-Life Case Studies for School Board Members, So You Want to Become a College Professor?, So You Want to Become a Principal?,* and *Are We Still a Nation at Risk Two Decades Later?*